BARBARIANS IN GREEK TRAGEDY

BARBARIANS IN GREEK TRAGEDY

by Helen H. Bacon

Published for Smith College
by the Yale University Press

New Haven, 1961

Printed in the United States of America.
Library of Congress catalog card number: 61-6665

To Henry, Deborah, John, Missy, Hugh

ACKNOWLEDGMENTS

To Richmond Lattimore, for his patient and penetrating criticism of my manuscript, and to Lily Ross Taylor, for her generous and imaginative encouragement of the undertaking, go my particular thanks. Chief among the many others who have been responsible for improvements in the form or content of this study I would like to name with gratitude: Agnes K. Michels, T. R. S. Broughton, Laurence Stapleton, and Mabel Lang of Bryn Mawr College; the late Karl Lehmann of the Institute of Fine Arts of New York University; Pauline Walker of Northampton, Massachusetts; George and Mary Dimock, Louis and Athena Cohn-Haft, Edward Spofford, John Herington, and Jean Oppenheimer of Smith College; Emma Kaplan and Catherine Blizzard of the Smith College Library; John Moore of Amherst College; Bernard Knox of Yale University; Julia McGrew of Vassar College; Marian Ash of the Yale University Press.

I would also like to thank Smith College for its sponsorship of my book; the American School of Classical Studies at Athens and the American Academy in Rome for their hospitality during the year abroad when a large part of it was written; the Fulbright Commission, which financed that visit; and the Ford Foundation, which has contributed to the cost of publication.

H. H. B.

CONTENTS

ABBREVIATIONS

Boisacq	Émile Boisacq, *Dictionnaire Étymologique de la Langue Grecque*, 4th ed. Heidelberg, 1950.
Darem.-Sag.	Ch. Daremberg, Edm. Saglio, *Dictionnaire des Antiquités Grecques et Romaines d'après les Textes et Monuments*, Paris, 1877–1919.
Frisk	Hjalmar Frisk, *Griechisches etymologisches Wörterbuch*, fascicles 1–9, Heidelberg, 1954–59.
L & S	*A Greek-English Lexicon*, edited by H. G. Liddell and R. Scott, new ed. revised by H. S. Jones and R. McKenzie, 2 vols. Oxford, n.d.
Pearson	*The Fragments of Sophocles*, edited by A. C. Pearson, 3 vols. Cambridge, 1917.
PW	*Real-Encyclopädie der classischen Altertumswissenschaft*, edited by A. Pauly, G. Wissowa, W. Kroll, Stuttgart, 1894– .

Schmid-Stählin Wilhelm Schmid, Otto Stählin, *Geschichte der griechischen Literatur*, Part I, 5 vols. Munich, 1929–48.

TGF *Tragicorum Graecorum fragmenta*, edited by A. Nauck, 2nd ed. Leipzig, 1889.

The abbreviations of the titles of the extant plays of Aeschylus, Sophocles, and Euripides are those of the *Oxford Classical Dictionary*.

The Oxford Classical Dictionary has also been my model for the English spelling of Greek names. When, as in the case of titles of some of the lost plays, it provides no model, and no accepted English spelling exists, I have transliterated.

The text of quotations from the extant plays is that of the Oxford Classical Text editions of Gilbert Murray for Aeschylus and Euripides, of A. C. Pearson for Sophocles.

Unless otherwise specified the text of quotations from the fragments is that of *TGF*. In the case of Sophocles, when it is necessary to distinguish between the text of Nauck and the text of Pearson, N following the fragment number indicates Nauck, P following the fragment number indicates Pearson, e.g. Sophocles fr. 432 P *Momos* = *fr.* 390 N. The title of the play, when known, is given after the number of the fragment. If the title is not known this is indicated by inc. (= incertum) after the number of the fragment. For very long fragments a line number is given after the title, e.g. fr. 314 P *Ichneutae*, 300.

1. INTRODUCTORY

Limits of the study

The largely quantitative observations of this study are not presented as a substitute for literary criticism. What follows is mainly an attempt to establish facts—to find out how much, and in what ways, Aeschylus, Sophocles, and Euripides used the knowledge of their own day in representing foreigners. Until now no one has attempted to collect all the references from plays and fragments and consider them together, in order to see what they can tell us. We have had mainly generalizations about the treatment of foreigners by the three tragedians, based on a few passages from the extant plays, usually considered out of context. A few special studies have dealt more thoroughly with one or another very limited aspect of the subject.

To determine the facts I have examined in detail the representation of foreign people and places by each writer; that is, the way the dramatists portray cultural, as opposed to personal, characteristics of barbarians. The fifth century had a good deal of information, some more, some less reliable, about the foreign peoples of Greek mythology. Aeschylus, Sophocles, and Euripides, each in his own way, make use of this material in representing foreign characters and scenes. They apply contemporary information about foreign language, physical appearance, costume, objects, customs and manners, geography, to the barbarians of the traditional stories. They differ significantly both in the manner and the extent to which they do this. This study lists and discusses the various kinds of information each of the dramatists has about foreigners, and the ways in which he uses this information.

Of course a complete separation of fact from literary interpretation is not possible, but this study confines itself as much as it can to the facts and some of their more immediate implications. It barely touches on the more complex and far-reaching questions of interpretation which the establishing of these facts raises. When I speak of "facts" I refer to what the authors do with what they think of as facts. I am not so much concerned to discover whether they have accurate knowledge about foreign peoples and places, as with whether they have tried to have accurate knowledge. It would take several specialists to verify their data thoroughly, and in some cases verification would be impossible because the evidence is lacking. From the literary point of view what is important is whether the writer creates a vaguely exotic effect, or a detailed, concretely visualized picture of some specifically foreign person, place, or thing; whether he indiscriminately applies to all that is not Greek a few formulae suggesting strangeness, or gives the foreign element specific qualities which were thought to be characteristic of one nationality and of no other.

The reader will find this literal enumeration of facts with a minimum of interpretation less restricting and distorting if he will bear in mind a few literary distinctions which are important, though they are not developed in my discussion. I have called the concrete and specific treatment of foreign material "realistic," since it presents an illusion of reality. Yet it may also be symbolic, and either consciously or unconsciously inaccurate. Xerxes' quiver (*Pers.* 1020–25) is a realistic detail, one of the characteristic insignia of the Great King (see below, p. 33 with n. 16). But the reference to its emptying makes it part of a complex of symbols of outpouring, squandering, draining, which are both an emotional and a moral statement about Xerxes. Io's journey (*PV* 706–41, 790–818) can be plotted on the scientifically conceived map of the Ionian physicists (see below, p. 49 with n. 43), but it is also a symbol of the mind's capacity to annihilate space, and, I think, of woman as preserver of and link with the past, as Heracles' western journey (fr. 195–9 *PL*) is a symbol of man as discoverer and explorer of the future. To give Persian traits to Trojans of the heroic age, as Sophocles does (see below, pp. 101–4), though anachronistic and historically incorrect, is also a form of realism. The Trojans become "real" foreigners, possible people, concretely Persians, instead of vaguely non-Greeks. I have limited myself to demonstrating that the three writers' treatment of foreign people and places is or is not "realistic" in this sense. The literary and artistic implications of symbolic, anachronistic, and other kinds of realism I have left for a later and less exclusively factual study.

Again, geographical formulae, involving both Greek and foreign places—Tyrrhenian trumpets, Scythian iron, Thracian winds, Laconian hounds—occur throughout Greek drama, and therefore are in some sense stock expressions. They are not in all cases, however, used in a purely decorative, that is Alexandrian, manner. In *Antigone*, for example, Thrace, the home of Ares and Dionysus, opposing forces in the play, unites in the image of the storm their similar, but contrary, forms of violence. To say that Sophocles uses the formula about Thracian winds does not suggest how he gives uniqueness to the stock expression by implicating it in the over-all imagery of the play. Aeschylus does something similar with Scythian iron in *Seven Against Thebes* (see below, pp. 36–8). My discussion only occasionally, and in passing, touches on the different ways of using such formulae.

The richest and most complex of all the aspects of the subject has also barely been suggested. That is the use of the conflict of Greek and barbarian as a theme —a question always in the background when religion, customs, and manners are being considered. I have limited myself to pointing out that the theme exists, even in Sophocles, and that it is not, in any of the writers, a simple question of superior Greek against inferior barbarian. The tendency to associate barbarians with slaves, women, and other victims of society, as well as with tyrants and primitives, noble or debased, the relation of barbarians to reason, passion, and self-control, both personal and public, and all this implies for good and evil about the Greeks they are involved with, and about the writers' attitudes toward Hellenism and the world in general, has been left for another study. This one stops where literary criticism begins. The facts, so simply enumerated, are perhaps more accessible than if they had been built into a more complexly literary study. It is my hope that they can be the basis of some new criticism of Greek tragedy both by myself and others.[1]

Definition of barbarian

The barbarian, of course, is the foreigner, the non-Hellene. In most cases Greek tradition leaves no doubt about who that is. Trojan, Persian, Egyptian, Lydian,

1. Mathematical precision in dealing with literature creates an illusion of accuracy which is not attainable or significant. Even in a quantitative study like this, one reference or title more or less does not significantly alter the general picture. I have not therefore attempted absolute accuracy in the lists and statistics on which my discussion is based. My figures are approximate, based on available current information. Some references—particularly in recently discovered fragments—and many discussions about the content or authenticity of lost plays, will have escaped me. Because of the uncertainty over the authorship of *Rhesus* I have not included it in any part of my investigation. Its inclusion or exclusion does not make any important difference to the results of my study.

Taurian are always βάρβαροι in Greek literature. But in the case of border states, like Macedon, and some of the islands, like Lemnos, it is not always perfectly clear whether the Greeks considered them Hellenic or not. In order to avoid confusion and contradiction I have taken as a rough standard of what constitutes a Greek mainland state Aeschylus' description of Pelasgus' realm (*Supp.* 254–61).[2] This includes the coast west from the Strymon, the Perrhaebi—but not the Paeonians or Macedonians—the lands beyond Pindus to Dodona, and therefore presumably Aetolia, Acarnania, and Ambracia. It seems a not too arbitrary assumption that Aeschylus, in assigning this, in Greek terms, huge realm to Pelasgus, was trying to suggest some common prehistoric relationship which justified regarding this group of lands as a cultural unit. All these peoples I have treated as Greeks except on the few occasions when there is some clear indication that the author is, for the moment, giving them foreign traits, e.g., the Aetolian Tydeus of *Seven* and *Phoenissae* (*Sept.* 386 and *Phoen.* 132–40; see below, p. 32 with n. 15). There is no indication that the plays dealing with the Meleager saga treated the Aetolians as barbarians. Nor do we have any proof that Aeschylus treated the Perrhaebi as foreigners in his lost play *Perrhaebides* (fr. 184–6).

For the islands, it seems fairly certain that Cyprus was a foreign place (Aesch. *Supp.* 277–88); and both Herodotus (1.171–3; 7.169–71) and Sophocles thought

2. Cf. W. Kranz, *Stasimon* (Berlin, 1933), p. 79.

Cretans were barbarians, at least in prehistoric times.[3] Lemnos was still partly foreign even in Herodotus' time (5.26–7; 6.136–40; 8.11). I have accordingly treated these three islands as foreign places.

Names like Cilissa—the nurse in *Choephoroe*—as well as such information as we have about the population of Greece, suggest that slaves are usually of foreign descent.[4] But many, like the herdsman of *Oedipus* (*OT* 1123), can be assumed to have been born and brought up in a Greek household. I have therefore included slaves in my study only when, like the Phrygian of *Orestes*, or the chorus of *Choephoroe*, they are given special foreign characteristics.

Choice of subjects

As far as we can tell, no one of the three dramatists has a special predilection for myths dealing with foreigners. Statistics based largely on the titles of lost plays are inevitably shaky, but, such as they are, they indicate that slightly less than half the titles of each author probably involved foreign characters, or settings,

3. Cf. Schmid-Stählin, I^2, 433. When Agamemnon accuses Teucer of being half-barbarian Teucer answers (*Ajax* 1291–5),

> οὐκ οἶσθα σοῦ πατρὸς μὲν ὃς προὔφυ πατὴρ
> ἀρχαῖον ὄντα Πέλοπα βάρβαρον Φρύγα; . . .
> αὐτὸς δὲ μητρὸς ἐξέφυς Κρήσσης.

4. Cf. Schmid-Stählin, I^3, 695, and Aubrey Diller, *Race Mixture among the Greeks before Alexander*, Illinois Studies in Language and Literature, *20* (Urbana, 1937), 119.

or both.[5] If there are differences in approach then, they will be not in choice of stories, but in manner of handling stories about foreigners. The choice of myths about foreigners is not determined by the special tastes

5. Of the 79 surviving titles of Aeschylus we can be fairly sure that the following 34 had a foreign setting or foreign characters, or both (see A. Dieterich in PW, *1*, 1059–73): 29 of the lost plays, *Aegyptii*, *Aetnaeae*, *Amymone*, *Argo*, *Bassarai*, *Cabiri*, *Cares*, *Cressae*, *Danaides*, *Edoni*, *Heliades*, *Hoplon Krisis*, *Hypsipyle*, *Lemniae*, *Lycurgus*, *Memnon*, *Myrmidones*, *Mysi*, *Nereides*, *Niobe*, *Palamedes*, *Pentheus*, *Philoctetes*, *Phorcides*, *Phryges*, *Prometheus Luomenos*, *Proteus*, *Psychostasia*, *Threissae;* 5 of the extant plays, *Suppliants*, *Persae*, *Prometheus*, *Agamemnon*, *Choephoroe*. Of the 130 surviving titles of Sophocles, of which somewhere between 7 and 17 are probably spurious, the following 49 probably had a foreign setting or foreign characters or both (see A. v. Blumenthal in PW, *3* A, 1050–79 and Schmid-Stählin, I², 325): 47 of the lost plays, *Aechmalotides*, *Aethiopes*, *Aias Lokros*, *Alexander*, *Amycus*, *Andromache*, *Antenoridae*, *Chryses*, *Colchides*, *Eurypylus*, *Helenes Apaitesis*, *Helenes Harpage*, *Hippodamia*, *Iberes*, *Kamikoi*, *Kophoi Satyroi*, *Lacaenae*, *Laocoon*, *Lemniae 1 & 2*, *Manteis*, *Memnon*, *Minos*, *Mysi*, *Nausicaa* or *Pluntriae*, *Oenomaus*, *Palamedes*, *Phaeacians*, *Phaedra*, *Philoctetes in Troy*, *Phineus 1 & 2*, *Phryges*, *Poimenes*, *Polyxena*, *Priam*, *Rhizotomoi*, *Scythae*, *Sinon*, *Tantalus*, *Teucer*, *Tereus*, *Thamyras*, *Triptolemus*, *Troilus*, *Xoanephoroi;* 2 of the extant plays, *Ajax* and *Philoctetes*. Of the 74 surviving titles of Euripides the following 33 probably had a foreign setting or foreign characters or both (see Schmid-Stählin I³, 329–30. *Rhesus*, *Pirithous*, *Rhadamanthys*, *Tennes*, *Cadmus*, and *Mysi* are excluded as not genuine): 22 of the lost plays, *Aegeus*, *Alexander*, *Andromeda*, *Archelaus*, *Bellerophon*, *Busiris*, *Chrysippus*, *Cressae*, *Cretes*, *Epeius*, *Erechtheus*, *Hippolytus*, *Hypsipyle*, *Oenomaus*, *Palamedes*, *Peliades*, *Phaethon*, *Philoctetes*, *Polyidus*, *Protesilaus*, *Syleus*,

of the writer, but by the nature of mythology.[6] The relation of Greeks and non-Greeks is such a universal theme of Greek mythology that it cannot be avoided by writers who use mythology as the principal source of their plots.

The word βάρβαρος

There are differences of approach, of course. Anyone who reads the extant plays must observe Aeschylus' delight in exotic effects, Euripides' interest in violent foreigners, and the apparent lack of both concerns in Sophocles. There are other less immediately obvious differences. If we look at the way in which the three writers use the word *βάρβαρος* we find suggestions that Euripides has a special approach that sets him apart from Sophocles and Aeschylus. Since there are

---

Theseus; 11 of the extant plays, *Hippolytus, Medea, Andromache, Hecuba, Troiades, Bacchae, Helen, Electra, Orestes, Phoenissae, IT.* The actual number of plays with foreign characters or setting is probably higher since, of the lost plays, I have listed only those where the myth itself, or the contents of the fragments, or comments of ancient readers, leave little doubt about the presence of foreign material. I have not attempted to deal with the conjectures and reconstructions of modern scholarship.

6. There is an interesting discussion of foreigners in Greek mythology in Diller, *Race Mixture*, pp. 32–56. Diller does not discuss speculative myths about foreign peoples—such as adventures with Colchians, Arimaspians, etc.—but limits himself to stories that throw light on Greek ideas about the composition of the Hellenic race.

many more plays and fragments of Euripides than there are of Sophocles and Aeschylus it is not particularly significant if a word used by all three writers occurs most frequently in Euripides, unless there is a very marked disproportion. This is the case with *βάρβαρος*. There are two and a half times as many extant plays of Euripides as there are of Sophocles and Aeschylus, but he uses *βάρβαρος*, or a related word, ten times as often as Sophocles, six times as often as Aeschylus.[7] This suggests that, regardless of the relative number of foreign characters and settings in the three writers, the fact of foreignness is more important to Euripides than it is to Aeschylus and Sophocles.

Euripides has also indicated his special emphasis by extending the meaning of the word. It has three chief meanings in all three writers: (1) unintelligible, (2) foreign, non-Greek, referring simply to nationality, (3) foreign, with some implication of inferiority.[8] All

7. According to my count the figures are Aeschylus 18 (extant plays, *βάρβαρος* 14, *κάρβανος* 4, fragments 0), Sophocles 11 (extant plays, *βάρβαρος* 6, *βαρβαρόω* 1, fragments, *βάρβαρος* 4), Euripides 110 (extant plays, *βάρβαρος* 101, *βαρβαρόω* 1, *μειξοβάρβαρος* 1, fragments, *βάρβαρος* 7). I have checked these figures against Gabriel Italie, *Index Aeschyleus* (Leiden, 1955); F. Ellendt, *Lexicon Sophocleum* (2d ed. Berlin, 1872); James T. Allen and Gabriel Italie, *A Concordance to Euripides* (Berkeley and Los Angeles, 1954).

8. A bibliography, and the best and fullest study of the word and the concept, is given by Julius Jüthner, *Hellenen und Barbaren, aus der Geschichte des Nationalbewusstseins*, (Das Erbe des Alten, Vol. 8, new series, Leipzig, 1923). The only later discussion I have found is the brief and intelligent

three senses were current at the same time. They can be found, for instance, in Aeschylus, *Seven* 463,

φιμοὶ δὲ συρίζουσι βάρβαρον βρόμον,

of the bridle of the horses of the Argive Eteocles; in *Suppliants* 118,

καρβᾶνα δ' αὐδὰν εὖ, γᾶ, κοννεῖς,

the Danaids referring to their native language; in *Agamemnon* 919–20,

μηδὲ βαρβάρου φωτὸς δίκην
χαμαιπετὲς βόαμα προσχάνῃς ἐμοί,

---

one in Diller (*Race Mixture*, p. 21). There are three principal earlier studies: Friederich Roth, *Bemerkungen über den Sinn und Gebrauch des Wortes Barbar* (diss. Nürnberg, 1814); Arno Eichorn, *βάρβαρος quid significaverit* (diss. Leipzig, 1904); Hans Werner, "Barbarus," *Neue Jahrbuch für das klassische Altertum, 41* (1918), 389–408. There seems to be no disagreement about the history and meanings of the word. It is originally an onomatopoeic word imitating any kind of unintelligible sound, whether of animal, object, or man. Boisacq and Frisk derive it from Sanskrit *barbarah.* Boisacq relates it to Greek *βαβαί*, *βαβάζειν*, and Latin *balbus, balbutio.* Its second meaning—foreign, non-Greek—is a natural application of the fact that foreign speech sounds like stuttering, or simply meaningless noises, to those who do not know the language. In its third sense—foreign with some connotation of inferiority—no personal baseness is implied, but there is a suggestion, for instance in the carpet scene of *Agamemnon* or Apollo's tirade against the furies in *Eumenides* (185 ff.), that Greek customs are superior to barbarian ones. All the writers I have mentioned agree that this third sense coincides with the intensification of national consciousness and the corresponding hostility toward outsiders that arose during the struggle with Persia.

Agamemnon objecting to the carpet. It is important to observe that though Agamemnon disapproves of the servile foreign custom there is no implication here, or anywhere else in Aeschylus, that barbarians or their customs as such are intrinsically inferior. Darius has all the "Greek" virtues. Cassandra is morally superior to Clytemnestra. In Euripides this third meaning is sometimes extended to include intrinsic moral inferiority. Occasionally in Euripides it loses all reference to nationality and means *only* savage, evil, cruel, etc.[9] Jason expresses this idea (*Medea* 1339–40) though he does not actually use the word, when he attributes Medea's unnatural savagery against father, brother, and children to her foreign origin and adds,

9. Eichorn (*βάρβαρος quid significaverit*, pp. 34–7) gives the following examples of this meaning: *Andr.* 243, 261; *Tro.* 764; *Hec.* 326 ff, 1129, 1247 ff; *Medea* 1323 ff; *Heracl.* 131; *IT* 31, 389, 417, 739, 886; *Or.* 1110 ff, 1351, 1369 ff; *Helen* 501, 1210; *Phoen.* 497–8. In these passages, he points out, the word has a primarily ethical sense. Depending on the context, it can mean wicked, savage, shameless, pitiless, effeminate, lecherous. I am inclined to think the passage from *Phoenissae*, which he uses as an example of the intellectual inferiority of barbarians, is not a case in point. The chorus's comment on Polyneices' defense of his actions is,

ἐμοὶ μέν, εἰ καὶ μὴ καθ' Ἑλλήνων χθόνα
τεθράμμεθ', ἀλλ' οὖν ξυνετά μοι δοκεῖς λέγειν.

The reference need not be to intelligence, but to the difficulty of understanding caused by differences in language and custom. In any case, the word βάρβαρος is not used. The sum of the qualities conveyed by these passages must represent *a* contemporary Greek view of foreigners, *not necessarily*, as Eichorn is careful to point out, Euripides' own.

> οὐκ ἔστιν ἥτις τοῦτ᾽ ἂν Ἑλληνὶς γυνὴ
> ἔτλη ποθ᾽.

Word and idea coincide when Andromache curses the Greeks for dooming Astyanax (*Tro.* 764–5),

> ὦ βάρβαρ᾽ ἐξευρόντες Ἕλληνες κακά,
> τί τόνδε παῖδα κτείνετ᾽ οὐδὲν αἴτιον;

Βάρβαρα κακά *can* be translated "evils for barbarians," but the passion of her words and the brutality of the crime suggest that it means (what one instinctively wants it to mean) "savage evils." This is in keeping with the irony of the play in which the savages are not the Trojans but the Greeks. Used in this way, as Eichorn in his study of the word points out, it has lost all but its ethical meaning. Another example of this usage occurs in *Hecuba* (1129–31). The blinded Polymestor, in an insane rage, is trying to get hold of Hecuba and murder her. Agamemnon says to him,

> ἴσχ᾽. ἐκβαλὼν δὲ καρδίας τὸ βάρβαρον
> λέγ᾽, ὡς ἀκούσας σοῦ τε τῆσδέ τ᾽ ἐν μέρει
> κρίνω δικαίως ἀνθ᾽ ὅτου πάσχεις τάδε.

What can τὸ βάρβαρον be here but murderous desire? It only lacks the irony of the *Troiades* passage because it is addressed to a barbarian by a Greek.

The discussion that follows indicates that this rather striking contrast in the use of βάρβαρος between Euripides and his two predecessors is not accidental, but an index of a basic difference in point of view about the dramatic uses and importance of the foreign element in Greek mythology. When we examine in detail the way each writer deals with foreign language, physical appearance, costume, objects, customs and manners, the nature of this difference begins to appear.

2. AESCHYLUS

Language

Both foreign accents and foreign words are a usual part of Aeschylus' characterization of non-Greeks. In *Suppliants* and *Persae* he reminds his hearers by frequent use of cacophonous effects and foreign words that his characters speak a foreign language. Some of the more spectacular cases of cacophony are the speech of the Egyptian herald (*Supp.* 825–902), which, as far as the text will permit us to read it, sounds quite un-Greek; [1] and the passages containing the great lists of Persian names. The iteration of non-Greek sounds in these lists gives the impression that the chorus is speak-

1. J. H. Heinrich Schmidt (*Die Eurythmie in den Chorgesängen der Griechen* [Leipzig, 1868], p. 306) and Johannes Oberdick (in his edition of *Suppliants* [Berlin, 1869], p. 198) both suggest that the hopeless condition of the text is due to the presence of Egyptian words. The only ones that can be detected however are the familiar βᾶρις (836, 873, 882) and the emendation χάμψα (878). Schmid (Schmid-Stählin, I², 291, n. 7) calls the herald's language broken Greek. O. Krausse (*De Euripide Aeschyli instauratore* [diss. Jena, 1905], p. 207) also thinks the corruptions are due to the use of strange or genuinely foreign words.

ing a foreign language. There are many other examples.

The Danaids refer directly to their strange speech. (*Supp.* 118–19),

ἱλεῶμαι μὲν Ἀπίαν βοῦνιν,
καρβᾶνα δ' αὐδὰν εὖ, γᾶ, κοννεῖς.

In 972–3 the chorus speak of foreigners as ἀλλόθροοι. A lost play (fr. 328 inc.) actually named a foreign tongue, Αἰθίοπα φωνήν. Another lost play used χελιδονίζειν in the sense of βαρβαρίζειν (fr. 450 inc.). Cassandra speaks

χελιδόνος δίκην
ἀγνῶτα φωνὴν βάρβαρον κεκτημένη

(*Ag.* 1050–1).[2] Perhaps Περσίδος γλώσσης ῥόθος (*Pers.* 406), though spoken by a Persian, is meant to suggest the harsh sounds of a strange tongue.

In *Suppliants* and *Persae* the foreign language effects are part of Aeschylus' plan to create an exotic scene by

2. E. Fraenkel (Aeschylus, *Agamemnon* [Oxford, 1950]) ad. loc. quotes, among other examples of this comparison, Hesychius, s.v. χελιδόνος δίκην (M. Schmidt's emendation of χελιδόσι, which does not fit the alphabetical order) τοὺς βαρβάρους χελιδόσιν ἀπεικάζουσιν διὰ τὸ ἀσύνετον (Wilamowitz' emendation of ἀσύνθετον), and the context of fr. 450, cited above, καὶ Αἰσχύλος τὸ βαρβαρίζειν 'χελιδονίζειν' φησί, καὶ Ἴων ἐν Ὀμφάλῃ (fr. 76 v. Bl.) τοὺς βαρβάρους χελιδόνας ἀρσενικῶς φησί, ὡς Ἡροδιανὸς κτλ. Cf. also Hdt. 2.57, πελειάδες δέ μοι δοκέουσι κληθῆναι πρὸς Δωδωναίων ἐπὶ τοῦδε αἱ γυναῖκες, διότι βάρβαροι ἦσαν, ἐδόκεον δέ σφι ὁμοίως ὄρνισι φθέγγεσθαι . . . ἕως δὲ ἐβαρβάριζε [ἡ γυνή], ὄρνιθος τρόπον ἐδόκεέ σφι φθέγγεσθαι.

every available means. The emphasis on foreign speech in *Agamemnon* is less expected. Aeschylus refers to it four times in Cassandra's relatively brief scene—going out of his way to stress this point. Clytemnestra knows that Cassandra's native language is not Greek (*Ag.* 1050–2), and fears that she may not understand Greek (*Ag.* 1060–1). In speaking of Troy the chorus use the word ἀλλόθροος (*Ag.* 1200).[3] Cassandra objects that the chorus should understand her better than they do because she knows Greek well, and incidentally explains to the audience how it is that she can talk to the chorus (*Ag.* 1254).

καὶ μὴν ἄγαν γ' Ἕλλην' ἐπίσταμαι φάτιν.

In the surviving plays of Sophocles and Euripides about Troy the question of how Greek and Trojan communicate is ignored, as it generally is in Homer. In the whole *Iliad* there are four passages suggesting that the Trojans and their allies do not speak Greek (2.802–6, 867; 3.2–3; 4.433–8).

The chorus of *Seven* uses ἑτερόφωνος of the Greek invaders. According to Bruno Snell this is because Aeschylus thinks of them as less civilized than the Thebans, therefore figuratively barbarians whose speech is unintelligible (see below, pp. 36–8).[4] But Aeschylus would not ask his audience to believe that

3. The text is uncertain, but it is clear that they refer to Cassandra's language as different from their own.

4. "Aischylos und das Handeln im Drama," *Philologus*, suppl. 20 (1928), 78 and n. 114.

Argives, Aetolians, and Arcadians were not Greeks. The word itself means only "speaking differently." I assume that Aeschylus refers to the differences in dialect between Boeotia and other parts of Greece, and therefore do not include ἑτερόφωνος in this discussion of references to foreign speech. Aeschylus' awareness of differences in dialect is proved by *Choephoroe* 563.

Aeschylus also uses actual foreign words in order to emphasize the foreignness of certain of his characters. Ἰᾶνες, which is used in various forms by the Danaids and Persians (*Supp.* 69; *Pers.* 178, 563, 899, 950, 951, 1011, 1025), though originally a Greek word (Ἴωνες) is known to be the name several Eastern peoples used for the Greeks.[5] There seems no reason to doubt that

5. Hesychius' statement, s.v. Ἴαννα (see Sophocles fr. 53 *Aechmalotides*), ἐν μὲν Αἰχμαλώτησι Σοφοκλέους ἀπέδοσαν Ἑλληνική· ἐπεὶ Ἴαννας τοὺς Ἕλληνας λέγουσιν. . . . ἐπιεικῶς δὲ οἱ βάρβαροι τοὺς Ἕλληνας Ἴωνας λέγουσιν . . . is confirmed by Lenschau's examples in PW (*9*, 1870, s.v. *Iones*), *jawan*, *jawnai*, and *yauna*, from Hebrew, Assyrian, and Persian documents respectively (see also H. Degen, *De Troianis scaenicis* [diss. Leipzig, 1900], p. 37). I do not therefore agree with Lattimore ("Aeschylus on the Defeat of Xerxes," *Classical Studies in Honor of William Abbott Oldfather* [Urbana, 1943], p. 91) that the recurrence of the word in *Persae* is primarily a sign of Aeschylus' pro-Athenian feelings, though I am convinced by his general thesis that the treatment of history in the play is best explained by Aeschylus' intention of keeping the spotlight on Athens' share in the Persian defeat. In treating Ἰᾶνες as a foreign word I follow Kranz (*Stasimon*, pp. 85 and 289). Max Pohlenz (*Griechische Tragödie* [2nd ed., Berlin, 1954], *1*, 62) while recognizing that Ἰᾶνες is used as a

Aeschylus knew this, and used the word to intensify the foreign atmosphere. Of actual foreign words Kranz lists the following nine "*als die markantesten*":[6]

> ἄγγαρος, a mounted Persian messenger (*Ag.* 282), a word of Assyrian origin, borrowed from the Persian (Hdt. 3.126; 8.98; Frisk and L & S, s.v.).

---

foreign word, believes that Aeschylus used it also to pay indirect tribute to Athens, the principal Ionian city.

6. *Stasimon*, p. 82, with accompanying notes. As far as I know the only other studies of foreign words in Aeschylus are those of W. B. Stanford (referred to below, n. 7 and 8). Schmid (Schmid-Stählin, I², 291) devotes only part of one footnote to the subject, and gives no bibliography. As examples of foreign words used by Aeschylus, Schmid gives the following five: βαλλήν, ἀγδαβάτης, καρβάν, μανδύη, πάλμυς, and the proper names of *Persae*. 'Αγδαβάτης (*Pers.* 924) may be a foreign word, or simply a textual corruption (see Italie, *Index Aeschyleus*, s.v. and Kranz, *Stasimon*, p. 88). Pohlenz (*Griechische Tragödie*, 2, 28) accepts Schütz' suggestion ἁβροβάται. F. R. Earp's chapter on "rare and epic words" in Aeschylus (*Style of Aeschylus* [Cambridge, 1948]) is not essentially a study of foreign words. Although he includes γλῶτται among "rare" words (p. 41), only three genuinely foreign words appear in his list: καρβάν, βοῦνις, βαλήν. His conclusion (pp. 44–5) that the number of "rare" words in a play does not depend in any important degree on the presence of barbarian characters is rendered doubtful by the indefiniteness of his lists, and by the fact that he does not mention the proper names of *Persae*. Wolfgang Aly (*De Aeschyli copia verborum* [diss. Berlin, 1906]) is concerned with dialect rather than foreign words. He names four words of foreign origin: ἀρβύλη, δέλτος, κάρβανος, πάλμυς. I have not considered the first two in my lists, since it is clear from their general usage that like χιτών, though borrowed from other languages, they have lost their foreign connotations.

βαλ(λ)ήν, lord (*Pers.* 657–8), either a Phrygian or a Thurian word (L & S, s.v.). Originates in Asia Minor (Frisk, s.v.).

βᾶρις, boat (*Supp.* 836, 873, 882; *Pers.* 553, 1075), an Egyptian word, according to Herodotus (2.41, 60, 96). Boisacq and Frisk (s.v.) derive it from Coptic *bari.*

βοῦνις, an adjective meaning hilly (*Supp.* 117, 129, 776), derived from βουνός, a Cyrenaic word (Hdt. 4.192, 199; Boisacq and Frisk, s.v. βουνός).

καρβάν or κάρβανος, for βάρβαρος (*Supp.* 118, 130, 914), an Egyptian or Hebrew word (Frisk, s.v.).

μᾶ (*Supp.* 890) and πᾶ (an emendation for βᾶ in *Supp.* 892), of Phrygian origin according to Kranz.

μανδύη, a woolen cloak (fr. 364 inc.), a Persian word (L & S, s.v. See below, pp. 30–1 with n. 14).

πάλμυς, king (fr. 437 inc.), an Asian or Lydian word (Boisacq and L & S, s.v.).

To these nine Stanford would add nine others.[7]

ἀγδαβάται (*Pers.* 924 and perhaps 960). The text is uncertain, and I cannot find that Stanford, or

7. W. B. Stanford, *Aeschylus and His Style* (Dublin, 1942), pp. 50–2. He notes that most of the examples are from *Suppliants* and *Persae*, and concludes, like Kranz, that they are one of Aeschylus' devices for characterizing foreigners (p. 52).

anyone else, is sure of the form or meaning for this word (see above, n. 6, p. 19).

βάκκαρις, incense (fr. 14 *Amymone*), a Lydian word (schol. *Pers.* 42; Frisk, s.v.).

βάσσαρα, a costume of the followers of Dionysus (fr. 59 *Edoni*, also the title of a lost play; see below, pp. 29–31 with n. 14), a Cyrenaic word according to Hesychius (s.v.).

βύσσινος, an adjective for fine linen, or cotton (*Pers.* 125; *Sept.* 1039), borrowed from the Egyptian via the Semitic (Boisacq and Frisk, s.v. *βύσσος*). Perhaps too generally known and used to have a strong foreign effect (e.g. Hdt. 2.86; 7.181; cf. *σινδών* below).

Δαριάν, *Δαριᾶνα* (*Pers.* 651, 663, 671), the Persian forms of Darius.

ὀᾶ (*Pers.* 117, 122, 570, 573, 578, 581), a Περσικὸν *θρήνημα*, according to the scholiast (ad loc.).

σίσυρνα or *σίσυρα*, a cloak of skin or hide (fr. 109 *Kerykes*), possibly a Thraco-Phrygian word (Hdt. 4.109; 6.67; Boisacq, s.v.).

σμίνθος, a mouse (fr. 227 *Sisyphus*), a Mysian word (schol. *Iliad*, 1.39. Boisacq, s.v. gives no foreign derivation).

χάμψα, crocodile (a probable correction in *Supp.* 878), an Egyptian word (Hdt. 2.60).

None of the investigators mentions the following:

μίτρα, an oriental headdress (quoted by Italie [*Index Aeschyleus* s.v.] from Papyrus Oxyrhynchus 2164, 1:30), probably an Asiatic word (Hdt. 1.125; 2.122; 6.90; Boisacq, s.v.).

σινδών, fine cloth (fr. 153 *Nereides*), an oriental loan word (Hdt. 1.200; 2.86, 95; 7.181; Boisacq, s.v.).

τιάρα, traditional Persian headdress (*Pers.* 661), a loan word of unknown origin (Hdt. 1.132; 3.12; 7.61; 8.120; Boisacq, s.v.).

Like βύσσινος these three words are perhaps too generally known and used to count as strange words, in spite of their foreign origin. The same would apply to αἴλινον (*Ag.* 121, 139, 169; Boisacq and Frisk, s.v.).

A certain outlandishness is also achieved by the use of unfamiliar words like κοννέω (*Supp.* 118, 130, 164). It is not always possible to know whether they are really foreign, or dialect, or simply rare.

There is a good tradition that Aeschylus used a great many Sicilian words. Thirty possible Sicilisms (many of them, however, Greek dialect rather than Italic) have been proposed, but the state of the evidence is such that we cannot be certain even of one.[8]

8. W. B. Stanford ("Traces of Sicilian Influence in Aeschylus," *Proceedings of the Royal Irish Academy*, 44, C 8, pp. 229 ff) gives an account of the tradition and the state of the evidence. The principal passage is Athenaeus 9, 402 B (quoted by Stanford, p. 19). After saying that Aeschylus uses the Sicilian word ἀσχέδωρος for the wild boar, he adds: ὅτι δὲ Αἰσχύλος διατρίψας ἐν Σικελίᾳ πολλαῖς κέχρηται φωναῖς

To all these types of foreign words must be added the forty-nine names of Persian princes (*Pers.* 20–58, 302–30, 955–1001). At least ten of these are genuinely Persian, while others may be made up to sound Persian.[9] With the exception of two from *Agamemnon*

Σικελικαῖς οὐδὲν θαυμαστόν. See also Kranz's brief statement (*Stasimon*, p. 88) and Stanford's résumé in *Aeschylus and His Style* (pp. 52–3).

9. Kranz (*Stasimon*, pp. 91–2) lists 49 names, after study of the text and all its variants. Of these, according to linguistic authorities (see Kranz's bibliography, p. 291), the following ten are indisputably Persian: Ariomardos, Arsakes, Arsames, Artames, Artaphrenes, Artembares, Megabates, Mitrogathes, Oibares, Pharnuchos. Many of the others could be Persian or Hellenized Persian. Kranz takes this as evidence that none of the names were invented by Aeschylus, and infers that Aeschylus had what he considered reliable historical evidence for his names. This does not of course rule out the possibility that one of his sources, oral or written, might have invented or altered names. Lattimore ("Aeschylus on the Defeat of Xerxes," pp. 84–8) gives a more complete idea of the degree and kind of accuracy we may expect from Aeschylus. After a detailed comparison of the names in Aeschylus with those in Herodotus 7–9, he concludes (p. 87) that even if most of the names are genuinely Persian, "the 'prosopography' of Persian chiefs in *Persae* is to a great extent fictitious, or at least historically insignificant and misleading." Aeschylus, he goes on to point out (pp. 87–8), could not kill off well-known Persians without violating known history. He compares the long lists of otherwise unknown warriors who fall before Hector in the *Iliad*. Homer, like Aeschylus, could not kill off famous heroes in defiance of "history." This explanation does not apply to the first catalogue (*Pers.* 20–58), which precedes the news of the Persian defeat, but it seems to me to give in general a satisfying description of how Aeschylus can be at once "historical" and "unhistorical."

and eight from the fragments, all the foreign words cited have come from *Persae* or *Suppliants*. Counting the names of *Persae* there are seventy-one foreign words in all.[10]

Aeschylus emphasizes the foreignness of his foreigners by having them and others remind us of their foreign speech, by cacophonous imitation of foreign speech, and by using actual foreign words. With the Danaids and the Egyptians, with Cassandra and the Persians, he reminds us, not occasionally but constantly, directly and indirectly, in dialogue and lyric, that Greek is not their native tongue. The language of his foreign characters is not a matter for an occasional reference, but a consistent part of their characterization—a concrete detail carefully established by the devices I have been discussing.

Physical appearance

Most of Aeschylus' references to the different physical characteristics of foreigners are in *Suppliants*. Pelasgus, on first seeing the Danaids, does not believe their claim that they are Argives. He guesses from their appearance that they are Libyans, or Egyptians, or

10. I have not included *οἶστρος* in my list of foreign words, though it would appear from *Suppliants* 308, *οἶστρον καλοῦσιν αὐτὸν οἱ Νείλου πέλας*, that Aeschylus thought it was an Egyptian word. However, since the editors are agreed that something has happened to the text at this point, we cannot be sure what Aeschylus meant by these words, or even if they are his own.

Cyprians, or camel-riding nomadic Indians who are neighbors of the Ethiopians, or flesh-eating bow-carrying Amazons (*Supp.* 277–90). They are darker than Argives, but apparently not black, since he compares them to peoples who are merely dark, as opposed to black—the neighbors of the Ethiopians, but not the Ethiopians themselves. Danaus also refers to the foreign appearance of his daughters (*Supp.* 496–8).

> μορφῆς δ' οὐχ ὁμόστολος φύσις.
> Νεῖλος γὰρ οὐχ ὅμοιον Ἰνάχῳ γένος
> τρέφει.

Both Danaus and his daughters describe their pursuers with the word μελάγχιμος (*Supp.* 719 and 745). When they call the herald a spider and a black dream, they are no doubt thinking of his dark skin, among other things (*Supp.* 887–8).

It is a question whether in *Persae* 247,

> τοῦδε γὰρ δράμημα φωτὸς Περσικὸν πρέπει μαθεῖν,

we have a description of a physical characteristic of Persians or not. No other remark in *Persae* distinguishes Greeks from Persians physically.

There are two other more general references. The Danaids describe themselves thus (*Supp.* 154–6),

> . . . μελανθὲς
> ἡλιόκτυπον γένος.

By using *ἡλιόκτυπον* they compare their blackness to that of negroes, who have, as it were, been burned black by the sun. In a lost play (fr. 370 inc.), *μελανστέρφων γένος* also seems to be a reference to a dark-skinned foreign people. The word occurs only here, and may be corrupt.

The darkness of the Egyptians is referred to often enough in *Suppliants* to be, like the strangeness of their speech, a consistent part of their characterization. We cannot infer much else about this topic. Aeschylus does not seem to have thought of Trojans and Persians as differing in physical appearance from Greeks. Apparently he distinguished between the merely dark Egyptians, Cyprians, etc., and the truly black Ethiopians. If the treatment of the Egyptians is to be taken as an indication, plays like *Memnon*, which dealt with other races, must have played up their different physical characteristics.[11]

Costume

Most of Aeschylus' references to foreign dress are, again, in *Suppliants* and *Persae*. Danaus, describing from a distance the pursuing Egyptians, sees the contrast between their traditional white garments and their dark skins (*Supp.* 719–20).

11. That Aeschylus' Memnon was an outlandish and memorable figure we can guess from Aristophanes, *Frogs* 973 (quoted below, n. 15; see also Kranz, *Stasimon*, p. 72).

πρέπουσι δ' ἄνδρες νήιοι μελαγχίμοις
γυίοισι λευκῶν ἐκ πεπλωμάτων ἰδεῖν.

The Danaids wear Sidonian garments (*Supp.* 121), of linen (*Supp.* 120, 134), and damask (*Supp.* 432). As we know from Thucydides (1.6), the traditional Greek garment was of wool. The more luxurious linen tunic, worn by Ionians and Asiatics, was abandoned by the Athenians in favor of wool when they became fully Hellenized. In more general terms the Danaids' dress is unGreek (*Supp.* 234–7).

ποδαπὸν ὅμιλον τόνδ' ἀνελληνόστολον
πέπλοισι βαρβάροισι κἀμπυκώμασι
χλίοντα προσφωνοῦμεν; οὐ γὰρ Ἀργολὶς
ἐσθὴς γυναικῶν οὐδ' ἀφ' Ἑλλάδος τόπων.

This is Pelasgus' first reaction to the crowd of foreign women. Aeschylus visualizes them dressed and ornamented with unGreek splendor.

In *Persae* Persian dress is distinguished from Greek dress in Atossa's dream, where there are two maidens (*Pers.* 182–3),

ἡ μὲν πέπλοισι Περσικοῖς ἠσκημένη,
ἡ δ' αὖτε Δωρικοῖσιν.

The contrast, of course, is between the seamless woolen πέπλος of the Dorians and the elaborately sewn, sleeved and flowing χιτών of the Persians.[12] Like

12. No conclusions can be drawn from the use of the word alone. Even in the passages cited on pp. 26 and 27 it is used of both Greek and foreign dress. F. Studniczka (*Beiträge zur*

the Egyptians the Persian women wear linen (*Pers.* 125), *βυσσίνοις δ' ἐν πέπλοις πέσῃ λακίς*. The hat and shoes of the king are distinguished specifically and accurately (*Pers.* 660–3).

> *κροκόβαπτον ποδὸς εὔμαριν ἀείρων,*
> *βασιλείου τιήρας*
> *φάλαρον πιφαύσκων.*

The chorus is summoning Darius. The *εὔμαρις* is the Persian shoe, the *τιήρα* the traditional headdress. The *φάλαρον* is the peak of the tiara, which ordinarily was limp and hung down, but kings wore it upright. This detail, at least, is accurate, even if, as Gow suggests, Aeschylus was ignorant about what the rest of the king's costume should be.[13]

Geschichte der altgriechischen Tracht, Abhandlungen des archäologischepigraphischen Seminares der Universität Wien, *6*, 1 [1886], 134) demonstrates that πέπλος and χιτών in the three dramatists are interchangeable words of indefinite meaning. For example, the robe Dejaneira sends to Heracles is sometimes πέπλος (*Trach.* 602, 674), sometimes χιτών (*Trach.* 580, 612, 769). But in Atossa's dream the Doric πέπλος is clearly the unsewn woolen dress of Sparta. A. S. F. Gow ("Notes on the *Persae* of Aeschylus," *J.H.S.*, 48 [1928], pp. 133–58) points out that it was necessary, as well as appropriate, for the Greek woman to wear this dress, since the alternative Ionian χιτών was almost indistinguishable from the dress of Persian women (p. 137; see also Amelung in PW, *3*, 2309 ff, s.v. χιτών).

13. "Notes on the *Persae*," p. 148. Gow also points out (p. 144) that there is no evidence that Aeschylus, or any other Greek artist or writer, knew that the real dress of the Persian king was not the traditional short tunic—with or without sleeves—and trousers, but a flowing robe with voluminous

In the fragments too Aeschylus shows knowledge of foreign dress. Besides a vague reference to Dionysus' foreign appearance and costume (fr. 61 *Edoni*), he

---

sleeves. He imagines Aeschylus would have dressed him in the first type of garment, and says that his silence about everything but hat and shoes is explained by the fact that trousers were too undignified for poetry, and the tunic too hard to describe, since it went by the same name as Greek dress, χιτών (p. 151). Andreas Alföldi ("Gewaltherrscher und Theaterkönig," *Late Classical and Mediaeval Studies in Honor of Albert Mathias Friend jr.* ed. Kurt Weitzman and others [Princeton, 1955], p. 51) identifies the εὔμαρις with the cothurnus. He believes that the εὔμαρις and all other parts of the stage king's dress were imitated from the actual costume of the Persian king, which was designed to make him appear taller and more imposing than his subjects. There is no evidence for what the cothurnus looked like, or for its use in the fifth century theatre (see T. B. L. Webster, *Greek Theatre Production* [London, 1956], pp. 37 and 45). The Phrygian slave of Orestes wears εὐμάριδες (*Or.* 1370), which indicates that they were not, for stage purposes, an exclusively royal kind of footwear. Alföldi names this passage without quoting it. The article tries to prove that it was the robes of the Persian king rather than the robes of the priest of Dionysus that were the model for the stage king's costume. Only that part of his theory which concerns the fifth century drama is relevant to my discussion. His contention that Aeschylus introduced this costume for all foreign kings, and all tyrants, Greek as well as foreign, and that Sophocles and Euripides continued the practice, lacks proof and is in conflict with such evidence as we have. According to this theory all kings with tyrannical leanings—Oedipus, Creon, Agamemnon, Lycus, Pentheus—would be attired like Xerxes and Darius. Only a constitutional monarch like Theseus or Demophon would be dressed as a Greek. Against this is, first, the fact that we have almost no evidence for stage practice in this period, but what there is suggests no such rigid formalization

mentions the bassara (fr. 59) in the same play, and the mandya (fr. 364 inc.). Our information about these

---

of costume as this before the fourth century (T. B. L. Webster, *Greek Theatre Production*, pp. 35–44). Second, this study shows that, in the plays, foreign dress, foreign objects, foreign words are rarely mentioned except as parts of the characterization of foreigners. Unless costuming adheres to the same principles such references lose their point. Agamemnon's falling off toward tyranny was probably indicated by a more than usually splendid costume, but this does not mean that he wore the full regalia of the Great King. If Pentheus were dressed as an oriental monarch, the point of his disgust with Dionysus' foreign ways would be destroyed. And yet he is one of the most tyrannical figures of Greek tragedy. Underlying Alföldi's theory is the identification of what is evil, backward, and uncontrolled with what is foreign. This is an idea of modern criticism (see below, pp. 37–8) rather than of ancient tragedy. Alföldi takes all references to luxury, tyranny, and ὕβρις as implying barbarian excess in contrast to Hellenic moderation. This is his reason for imagining all tyrants in foreign dress. Ὕβρις φυτεύει τύραννον, but there are Greek as well as barbarian forms of ὕβρις. Pentheus' tyrannical behavior is a rejection of the foreigner, not an imitation of him. It is a Greek rather than an oriental aberration to try to rope the bull of Dionysus, to bind the force of life with narrow and purely intellectual prescriptions. Alföldi's own examples do not support this simple antithesis of noble Hellene against base barbarian. Out of context his examples do seem to associate foreign and good with Greek. But how bitterly mistaken, to mention only one of the passages he cites, is Philoctetes' assumption that strangers in Greek dress are friends to be trusted (*Phil.* 223–4). Barbarians play a more complex role in tragedy than Alföldi's theory allows for. It is only by a real distortion of values that one can imagine an Oedipus, a Creon, or a Pentheus dressed as an oriental monarch.

garments is vague, but there is little doubt that they were both distinct and recognizably foreign types of dress.[14]

Though Aeschylus' references to foreign costume are relatively few, they show that he knew a good deal about different styles of national dress, and visualized his characters appropriately dressed. He did not think vaguely of a general barbaric costume, but specifically of white linen for the Egyptians, of the upright tiara for the Persian king, of the bassara for the Thracian maenads.

Objects

References to foreign objects in Aeschylus are few and uninformative. The Tyrrhenian trumpet (*Eum.*

14. For the bassara see Darem.-Sag., s.v., and PW, *3*, 103, s.v. *bassarai*. There seems to be no way of being certain whether it was the long many-colored Thracian tunic of the Bassarids, or the fox skin they wore over it, or both. Hesychius and others relate it to the Libyan word for fox, βασσάριον, reported in Herodotus 4.192. For the μανδύας, or μανδύη, see PW, *14*, 1046 s.v. Apparently it was a heavy wool cloak like a chlamys, meant to keep out rain. The weight of the evidence is in favor of its being a Persian word, though Aeschylus himself (fr. 364 inc.) calls it

Λιβυρνικῆς μίμημα μανδύης χιτών.

According to Alföldi ("Gewaltherrscher und Theaterkönig," p. 46) it is the sleeveless cloak, fastened with a brooch, which is seen in representations of Persian dignitaries and Jewish high priests, and was part of the stage king's dress (see above, n. 13).

567) is a stock part of the poetic vocabulary, not a piece of living information about a foreign people (see below, pp. 76 and 127). The Tyrian ship (*Pers.* 962) is in a similar category. It simply alludes to the fact that the Persian navy was Phoenician. The Egyptian navy in *Helen* is also Phoenician (see below, p. 128). Like the Tyrrhenian trumpet this is an anachronism in the heroic age, comparable to Sophocles' Trojans and Phrygians with the cultural traits of Persians (see below, pp. 101–4). The Sardian chariots with two and three poles (*Pers.* 47), and Xerxes' Syrian chariot (*Pers.* 84) are not further described. There seems to be no special information in these references.

The shield of Tydeus (*Sept.* 386) is certainly meant to be a foreign implement. Hung with jangling bells to inspire fear in the enemy, it gives color to Aeschylus' picture of Tydeus as only semi-civilized.[15] More spe-

15. Cf. the description of Tydeus in Euripides' *Phoenissae* (132–40), where Antigone calls him μειξοβάρβαρος. Thucydides also describes the Aetolians as semi-barbarous in their way of life and manner of fighting (1.5–6; 3.94–8). Bells and other means of inspiring fear through suggestion are characteristic of barbarians in tragedy. Sophocles (fr. 775 inc.) gives bell-hung shields to the Trojans. Aeschylus' description of Tydeus' shield,

> ὑπ' ἀσπίδος δ' ἔσω
> χαλκήλατοι κλάζουσι κώδωνες φόβον,

is almost echoed in the description of the frontlet of Rhesus' horses (*Rhesus* 306–8),

> Γοργὼν δ' ὡς ἐπ' αἰγίδος θεᾶς
> χαλκῆ μετώποις ἱππικοῖσι πρόσδετος
> πολλοῖσι σὺν κώδωσιν ἐκτύπει φόβον.

cific than any of these is a reference to the *τρίγωνος*, a polyphonic kind of Asiatic harp (fr. 78 *Thalamopoioi;* see below, pp. 76–7).

Aeschylus of course often mentions Persian weapons —slings, bows, swords—but without describing them or distinguishing them from Greek weapons.[16] The crimson carpet of *Agamemnon* is never described. We do not even know whether it was made at home or abroad. In fact, of objects, Greek or foreign, there is very little description in Aeschylus.

Rhesus' shield also has bells on it (*Rhesus* 383–5). We can infer from the description of Aeschylus in *Frogs* 973,

> *Κύκνους ποιῶν καὶ Μέμνονας κωδωνοφαλαροπώλους,*

that Aeschylus represented Memnon in similar trappings, with a towering crest, and bells on his horses' cheek pieces. There is a comprehensive discussion of bells on barbarian armor and harness in Walter Miller, *Daedalus and Thespis, The Contributions of the Ancient Dramatic Poets to Our Knowledge of the Arts and Crafts of Greece* (3 vols., New York, 1929–32), 2, 476–7.

16. The epithet *μαχαιροφόρος* (*Pers.* 56) which suggests the short Persian sword (see p. 68 of this study), may be an exception to this statement. Gow ("Notes on the *Persae*," p. 156) points out that Aeschylus' view of the bow as a symbol of Persia and the spear as a symbol of Greece (*Pers.* 86, 147, 239, 926) is oversimplified. Though the bow and quiver are the symbol of the king in Persian art, and often appear in representations of other Persians, "where a Persian . . . is represented in combat with his enemies, the spear is his regular weapon."

Religion, customs, manners

Particularly in *Suppliants* and *Persae*, Aeschylus shows specific knowledge of foreign institutions.[17] He refers to the Egyptian gods by Greek names, but in such a way as to show that he knows their Egyptian functions and attributes (e.g., *Supp.* 210–21).[18] Herodotus (2.156) attests his unique knowledge of Egyptian religion, saying that he alone of the poets knew a certain λόγος which caused him to call Artemis the daughter of Demeter.[19] Aeschylus has introduced an Egyptian motif into the Io story of *Suppliants*—impregnation by the breath of god, or rather by a combination of his breath and touch, ἐξ ἐπαφῆς κἀξ ἐπιπνοίας (*Supp.* 17; cf. also 44–5, 577).[20] He knows

17. A really detailed study of this subject, using all the available archaeological, anthropological, and historical data, would be another book. The most complete study to date is in Kranz, *Stasimon*, pp. 83 ff. I have necessarily limited myself to a brief description of some of the most striking examples, which must be in many respects a summary of Kranz's summary.

18. Kranz, *Stasimon*, pp. 102–3 and 294. By way of illustration I mention two of Kranz's examples. The Danaids associate the bird of Zeus with the sun's rays. This can only be the sun bird of the Egyptian Zeus, Ammon Re. They notice with astonishment that the Greek Hermes is different from their own Thoth.

19. For the correctness of this information see Kranz, *Stasimon*, p. 103.

20. Kranz, *Stasimon*, pp. 103–4 and 295. This Egyptian version of the virgin birth is discussed in E. Norden, *Die*

in detail about the cult of the Nile (*Supp.* 560, 854, 879, 1025).[21] He speaks of the drinking of beer and the eating of the byblus plant (*Supp.* 761, 953; cf. Hdt. 2.77). The Danaids, not understanding the Argive constitution, assume that Pelasgus has the powers of absolute kingship (*Supp.* 370–5). Aeschylus knows about Egyptian xenophobia (*Supp.* 893–4, 921–3; cf. Hdt. 2.79, 91). A fragment (373 inc.) refers to the trickiness of Egyptians.

While there is not quite so much of this kind of knowledge in *Persae*, nevertheless Aeschylus is informed about Persian institutions. He knows that the Persians worship mountains, rivers, sun, sky, and earth (*Pers.* 49, 205–9, 497–9; fr. 144 *Mysi*),[22] that they re-

---

Geburt des Kindes (Leipzig, 1924), pp. 76 ff. The breath of Ammon Re (Zeus) begets the child Horos on a mortal maiden. See also Eitrem in PW, *9*, 1732 ff.

21. Kranz, *Stasimon*, pp. 100–1.

22. Kranz, *Stasimon*, pp. 86–7. Since the Greeks also thought of rivers and mountains as holy, the evidence in the phrases ἱεροῦ Τμώλου (*Pers.* 49) and ῥέεθρον ἅγνου Στρύμονος (*Pers.* 497) is not unequivocal. But knowledge of specific belief and ritual cannot be questioned in *Persae* 497–9,

θεοὺς δέ τις
τὸ πρὶν νομίζων οὐδαμοῦ τότ' ηὔχετο
λιταῖσι, γαῖαν οὐρανόν τε προσκυνῶν.

Cf. Herodotus 1.131. The association of eagle, sun, and altar carrying sacred fire (*Pers.* 205–9) is common in contemporary Persian art, according to Gow, "Notes on the *Persae*," pp. 138–40.

gard their kings as gods, or like gods (*Pers.* 80, 150, 157, 634, 643, 711, 856).[23] A mark of the Persian in Aeschylus is the salaam, mentioned or implied four times in *Persae* (152, 499, 588, 694–6), once in *Agamemnon* (920),[24] where, as often in Greek tragedy (e.g., the Phrygian slave of *Orestes*), Persian customs are attributed to Trojans (see below, pp. 101–4). I have already mentioned the use of the bow in battle as a national characteristic of Persians in Aeschylus (see above, page 33 with n. 16).

It is more surprising to find barbarian behavior and a Greek reaction to it represented in *Seven* 375–99 (see above, pp. 17 and 32 with n. 15), a play which does not have the explicit confrontation of Greek and foreigner that occurs in *Suppliants* and *Persae*. Tydeus, the semi-barbarian, relies on noise and the terrifying design of helmet and shield to frighten the enemy. Eteocles' reply to the messenger's description (*Sept.* 397–9),

> κόσμον μὲν ἀνδρὸς οὔτιν' ἂν τρέσαιμ' ἐγώ,
> οὐδ' ἑλκοποιὰ γίγνεται τὰ σήματα·
> λόφοι δὲ κώδων τ' οὐ δάκνουσ' ἄνευ δορός,

reminds us of Brasidas' encouragement to his troops when they were betrayed by the Macedonians, and left facing the Illyrians alone (Thucydides 4.126–8).

23. We do not know whether the Persian kings in the time of Aeschylus were regarded as gods, or only as like gods. The problem is discussed by Kranz, *Stasimon*, p. 87 and Gow, "Notes on the *Persae*," p. 136.

24. Kranz, *Stasimon*, p. 87.

Brasidas, like Eteocles, points out that it takes more than terrifying sights and sounds to win a battle, and develops even more explicitly the contrast between the drunken courage of the barbarian and the disciplined and rational strategy of the Greek. Terror-inducing sounds and sights with their suggestions of barbarism are an important motif in *Seven.* All the attackers except Amphiaraus use noise and terrifying shield devices as weapons, and the chorus voices an equally noisy panic which Eteocles checks rather violently. The presence of this motif in a play which has no direct connection with foreign people or places calls for a word of comment.

Bruno Snell associates the emotionalism of both attackers and chorus with what he calls the "archaic-barbaric," and contrasts their lack of control with the Hellenic, male, *σωφροσύνη* of Eteocles.[25] Like Alföldi (see above, p. 28, n. 13), he tends to polarize good and bad around Greek and non-Greek. I do not think that Aeschylus sets up such an antithesis in this or any other play. He does not present the attackers as barbarians. Their strange and violent attributes emphasize that they are strangers, alien to Thebes, speaking a different dialect (see above, p. 17), and that their behavior is full of *ὕβρις*. But they are not, like the Persians of *Persae* or the Egyptians of *Suppliants*, given a set of traits belonging to a specific foreign nationality. And Eteocles is not a representative of Hellenic *σωφροσύνη*, any more than the Argives, Arcadians, and Aetolians

25. "Aischylos und das Handeln im Drama," pp. 78–95.

are barbarians. He is self-controlled in the face of the chorus's panic at the prospect of invasion, but, when he has the choice of confronting his own brother in single combat, or sending another champion, he is swept away by emotions blinder and more irrational than theirs. Aeschylus uses the storm as the image both of the attack on the city, which creates panic in the chorus, and of the curse on the house of Laius, which precipitates Eteocles' choice, as though to emphasize that Eteocles' initial self-control is illusory. The captain of the ship of state is not the captain of his soul, and the inner storm that whirls him to doom is also a kind of ὕβρις, as destructive and more unnatural than any storm from without that can assail the city of Thebes. The foreign motifs of the play dramatize not Hellenism but incest, by contrasting the war between strangers with the war between brothers, who are also children of incest. The reconciler of those who are κάρτα ὅμαιμοι (*Sept.* 940) is a Scythian stranger, ξένος . . . Χάλυβος Σκυθῶν ἄποικος (*Sept.* 727–8). The ultimate estrangement, death by mutual murder, is also the only possible reconciliation of strife born of the stifling closeness of incest. The foreign motifs are not a portrait of barbarians as such, nor a comment on them. They are a way of showing what it means to vanquish an alien invader who is also a brother.

In *Eumenides* Apollo, driving the furies from his shrine, associates them with certain, to the Greek mind, characteristically Persian forms of punishment (*Eum.* 185–95; cf. Hdt. 3.48, 125; 7.39; 8.104–6; 9.112).

οὔτοι δόμοισι τοῖσδε χρίμπτεσθαι πρέπει·
ἀλλ᾽ οὗ καρανιστῆρες ὀφθαλμωρύχοι
δίκαι σφαγαί τε, σπέρματός τ᾽ ἀποφθορᾷ
παίδων κακοῦται χλοῦνις, ἠδ᾽ ἀκρωνίαι
λευσμοί τε, καὶ μύζουσιν οἰκτισμὸν πολὺν
ὑπὸ ῥάχιν παγέντες. ἆρ᾽ ἀκούετε
οἵας ἑορτῆς ἔστ᾽ ἀπόπτυστοι θεοῖς
στέργηθρ᾽ ἔχουσαι; πᾶς δ᾽ ὑφηγεῖται τρόπος
μορφῆς. λέοντος ἄντρον αἱματορρόφου
οἰκεῖν τοιαύτας εἰκός, οὐ χρηστηρίοις
ἐν τοῖσδε πλησίοισι τρίβεσθαι μύσος.

But no one, I imagine, would maintain that the furies are alien figures. Their primitive, female, emotional violence turns out to be indispensable to the Athenian way of life. It is neither Greek nor not Greek, but the violence of life itself, which both creates and destroys. Aeschylus is too aware of the fundamental importance of these qualities to label them "un-Hellenic" in any context.

Further indications of the quality of Aeschylus' knowledge of foreign custom are verbal correspondences with foreign documents. For several of the phrases in Darius' summary of Persian history (*Pers.* 765–81), parallels can be found in the Behistun Inscription and other Persian documents.[26] The king's titles, δεσπότης δεσποτᾶν (*Pers.* 666), βασιλεὺς μέγας (*Pers.* 24), πατήρ (*Pers.* 663, 671) and θεομήστωρ (*Pers.* 655), and those of his nobles, χιλίαρχος (*Pers.*

26. Kranz, *Stasimon*, pp. 95–8.

304), ὀφθαλμὸς βασιλέως (*Pers.* 979), μυριόνταρχος (*Pers.* 314), μυριοταγός (*Pers.* 993), πιστός, πιστά, πιστώματα (*Pers.* 2, 171, 443, 528, 681, 979), παραστάται (*Pers.* 957), are all historical.[27]

When the Danaids (*Supp.* 855–7) describe the Nile as

> ἀλφεσίβοιον ὕδωρ,
> ἔνθεν ἀεξόμενον
> ζώφυτον αἷμα βροτοῖσι θάλλει,

they are close to the wording and ideas of extant Nile hymns. This is not coincidence. Aeschylus knew about such hymns, for he refers to them once directly (*Supp.* 1024–5).

> . . . μηδ' ἔτι Νείλου
> προχοὰς σέβωμεν ὕμνοις.[28]

Wilamowitz apparently was the first to observe that Clytemnestra's greeting to Agamemnon (*Ag.* 895–901), and parts of her last speech in that scene (*Ag.* 966–71), imitate, and even echo, an Egyptian hymn of praise.[29] As Kranz points out, to Agamemnon her words as well as her actions have a foreign flavor.[30]

27. Ibid., pp. 88 and 290–1. See also Gow, "Notes on the *Persae*," pp. 134, 152, 154.

28. Kranz, *Stasimon*, pp. 101 and 294. A translation of a Nile hymn may be found in James B. Pritchard, *Ancient Near Eastern Texts Relating to the Old Testament* (Princeton, 1955), pp. 372–3.

29. *Hermes*, *62* (1927), p. 287. Also discussed by Kranz, *Stasimon*, pp. 101–2 and 294.

30. Ibid., p. 102.

μηδὲ βαρβάρου φωτὸς δίκην
χαμαιπετὲς βόαμα προσχάνῃς ἐμοί.

It is characteristic of Aeschylus that this remark has a precise application. It is not just the extravagance of Clytemnestra's praises, but the phrases and style that are "barbarous." It intensifies the irony of the scene to know that Clytemnestra consciously uses a foreign style of speech, as she urges on Agamemnon a foreign style of behavior.

Signs of another kind of painstaking, if not necessarily scientific, research appear in the genealogy of the Persian kings (*Pers.* 765–81), of the Danaids (*Supp.* 315–23), of Heracles (*PV* 850–73), and in the accounts of the bridging of the Hellespont and Bosporus, and of Xerxes' campaign in Greece.[31]

31. The immense question of the sources and correctness of Aeschylus' historical information, whether Greek or foreign, is not one that I can go into here. It is clear that he intended to be accurate. The extent to which he succeeded is another and more complicated question. For example, Kranz (pp. 95–8) demonstrates that the genealogy of the Persian kings (*Pers.* 765–81) is the product, not of invention (*erfindung*), but of research (*erkundung*). While there is much that Aeschylus does not know about Persian history, his account echoes the language of Persian documents and reflects traditions known from other sources. Perhaps we may take this as a sample of his methods. It is also true that he distorts history when it suits him to do so. Lattimore points out ("Aeschylus on the Defeat of Xerxes," p. 91) that, whether for the sake of dramatic unity, or in order to glorify Athens, or both, he has subordinated every other major event of the Persian Wars to the battle of Salamis.

Scattered through the plays are other bits of information about foreign customs. Most vivid and circumstantial is in Prometheus' description of Io's journey (*PV* 709–11).

> Σκύθας δ' ἀφίξῃ νομάδας, οἳ πλεκτὰς στέγας
> πεδάρσιοι ναίουσ' ἐπ' εὐκύκλοις ὄχοις,
> ἑκηβόλοις τόξοισιν ἐξηρτυμένοι.

In a fragment (198 *PL*) he calls the Scythians ἱππάκης βρωτῆρες—eaters of mare's milk cheese. These two quotations contain some of the more striking facts about the Scythians recorded by Herodotus (4.2–22, 59–92, 121, 127). The phrase Σκυθῆς ὅμιλος (*PV* 417) seems to reflect the tradition recorded by Thucydides (2.97; cf. also Hdt. 4.81) of the vastness of the population of Scythia.

Edoni (fr. 57) describes the rites of the Thracian Cotyto in eleven lines, more savage and more onomatopoeic than anything in *Bacchae*.

> σεμνὰ Κοτυτοῦς ὄργι' ἔχοντες,
> . . . .
> ὁ μὲν ἐν χερσὶν
> βόμβυκας ἔχων, τόρνου κάματον,
> δακτυλόδικτον πίμπλησι μέλος,
> μανίας ἐπαγωγὸν ὁμοκλάν,
> ὁ δὲ χαλκοδέτοις κοτύλαις ὀτοβεῖ
> . . . .
> . . ψαλμὸς δ' ἀλαλάζει·
> ταυρόφθογγοι δ' ὑπομυκῶνταί

ποθεν ἐξ ἀφανοῦς φοβεροὶ μῖμοι,
τυπάνου δ' εἰκὼν ὥσθ' ὑπογαίου
βροντῆς φέρεται βαρυταρβής.

Even the wildest lyrics of *Bacchae* express human feelings, ecstasy, grief, hatred; these lines of Aeschylus contain no emotions, only undifferentiated *emotion*, expressed through rhythm and sound. They come as near as words can get to the savage frenzy induced by the bullroarer and the thundermaker. He writes as though he had been present at a Thracian tribal ceremony, and felt the rhythm of the drums begin to take possession of him. The fragment has the violence of authentic primitive ritual.[32] *Bacchae* transforms, though it does not weaken, this violence, with the restraints and graces of the Greek lyric tradition.

Much slighter, but interesting because they suggest the breadth of his information, are a reference to beer, this time apparently Thracian (fr. 124 *Lycurgus*), to the Phrygian goddess Adrasteia (fr. 158 *Niobe*),[33] to the fact that the Curetes got their name from their long hair (fr. 313 inc.), to the *Di Palici* of Sicily (fr. 6 and 7 *Aetnaeae*), to the *Gabii* who live without sin and without labor (fr. 196 *PL*).

32. This fragment, together with Strabo 10.470, are the principal sources for the rites of Cotyto. See Schwem in PW, *11*, 1549 ff, s.v. *Kotys*. It is typical of Aeschylus, as it is rare in Euripides, to provide material so precise and concrete that it can be used in this way. Compare the passages on the Scythians just quoted.

33. The reference to Adrasteia in *PV* 936 seems to be proverbial, and conveys no special information.

In addition to these specific and concrete kinds of information, there are, of course, many general, and somewhat more formulaic, references to foreign customs and manners in Aeschylus—particularly to the wealth, luxury, emotional violence, and lack of political freedom of Persians, Phrygians, and foreigners in general.[34] Such references have sometimes been interpreted as implying that Aeschylus thought of foreigners as naturally "inferior" to Greeks. I have already given some reasons for disagreeing with this view (see above, pp. 10–12 with n. 8). Aeschylus may criticize *a* foreigner or *a* foreign institution, but of inferiority as a natural characteristic of foreigners, nationally or individually, there is little talk in Aeschylus. It is implied directly in *Suppliants* (760–1 and 952–3), indirectly in *Agamemnon* (855–974), and nowhere else. As a theme it is not important.

In spite of his impressive learning, Aeschylus, like Herodotus, occasionally transfers Greek ideas or customs to foreign characters. The Danaids, for example, carry the olive branch like Greek suppliants.[35] In *Persae* the cult of the dead, the purification rites followed by Atossa, are as Greek as they are Persian.[36]

34. For example, the continual use of compounds of ἁβρός in *Persae*, discussed by Kranz, *Stasimon*, p. 84.

35. Since the problem of whose marriage customs, if any, apply to the Danaids, has not been settled, I have not discussed this point. See George Thomson, *Aeschylus and Athens* (London, 1941), pp. 301 ff.

36. Gow however ("Notes on the *Persae*," p. 138) thinks that these rites may be common to Greeks and Persians. He

Darius judges Xerxes by Greek standards. Probably neither Aeschylus nor his audience asked themselves whether other peoples thought differently from Greeks in these matters. The effect of foreignness would therefore not be disturbed by such inaccuracies. Aeschylus is not always accurate, but he has recognized the value of facts in representing foreign peoples, and tried to get them. Homer's assumption that there is only one kind of human society is one that Aeschylus does not make.

Geography

Certain geographical names, by frequent repetition in similar contexts, have become part of the stock language of tragedy. They are formulae, and by themselves convey no information, though in context they may be, like the Scythian iron of *Seven*, allusive or symbolic. Aeschylus has a good number of these—the Tyrrhenian trumpet (*Eum.* 567) already mentioned (p. 31 above); the various oriental styles of mourning (Cissian and Arian, *Cho.* 423; Mysian, *Pers.* 1054; Mariandynian, *Pers.* 939); Chalybian iron (*Sept.* 728–30; *PV* 132–3); Scythian iron (*Sept.* 728–30, 818); Scythian Ares (*Cho.* 161–2). But a less formulaic style is more usual.

A place by place study of geography in Aeschylus is still to be made, but enough has been done to show

---

refers to Strabo 15.733, where a similar ritual is ascribed to the Persians. See Kranz, *Stasimon*, p. 86.

the quality and extent of his knowledge.[37] His geographical information is detailed and enormous. In all he names 100 foreign peoples and places, from the sources of the Nile to the Rhipaean Mountains; from Ethiopia, where the sun rises, to Spain and Ocean Stream, beyond the Pillars of Hercules (see Appendix). Many of these places are mentioned only in passing, but often in such a way as to show that Aeschylus knows where they are, or what they are like, or both. He writes like a man with a map in front of him.

When he lists places he usually names them in geographical order, as though he were seeing them in front of him on a map. This is perhaps to be expected in the journey speeches (*Supp.* 558–61; *Pers.* 480–512; *PV* 707–41, 790–818; fr. 195–99 *PL*, Heracles' western journey; cf. also the route of the fire, *Ag.* 281–316), though the journey of Euripides' Bacchic train is not so easy to follow (see below, p. 164).[38] But even

37. Sam Lee Greenwood's *Geographical Allusion in Attic Tragedy* (diss. Chicago, 1938) is incomplete and inconclusive. He neglects the fragments and the work of other scholars, and avoids any kind of critical evaluation of the material. His assertion (p. 9) that Sophocles has proportionately less geographical material than Euripides or Aeschylus overlooks the richness of Sophocles' fragments in this kind of material, and the largely formulaic nature of geographical references in Euripides (see below, pp. 94–101 and 155–67). His discussion of Greek opinion of barbarians takes every unfavorable comment at its face value, regardless of the speaker or the context, with the result that he pictures all three tragedians as jingoists.

38. See Kranz, *Stasimon*, pp. 79–81 for a general discussion

when no journey is involved Aeschylus, as though unable to separate his mind from a concrete image of the world, prefers to name places in geographical order; for example, the boundaries of Pelasgus' realm (*Supp.* 254–9);[39] and Darius' Greek tributaries, named not consecutively but in their natural geographical groupings (*Pers.* 865–96);[40] and the nations that mourn for Prometheus (*PV* 411–30), which are named from east

---

of journey speeches and other kinds of geographical description in Aeschylus.

39. Ibid., p. 79. The boundaries of Pelasgus' realm coincide roughly with those of mainland Greece in Aeschylus' own day, as though Aeschylus were presenting a mythological precedent for the distribution of Greek power on the mainland. In listing the territories that bound this kingdom Aeschylus moves from east to west, and then south, as though he were in fact describing a journey—Strymon, the Perrhaebi of Thessaly, the lands beyond Pindus as far as Paeonia, Dodona, the western sea, and Peloponnese.

40. Kranz (pp. 79–80) shows how systematic the description is. Aeschylus deals with the following districts: (1) Thrace, the lake dwellers and the mainland towns; (2) Hellespont, Propontis, Bosporus; (3) the islands, first Lesbos, Samos, and Chios, then the Cyclades from south to north, then Lemnos and Icaria "between the two coasts," then Cyprus with her cities; (4) the Ionian coast. Gow ("Notes on the *Persae*," p. 154) points out that there is a rough correspondence with the tribute districts of the Delian League, as they are known from 443 B.C. on—*ἐπὶ Θράκης*, *Ἑλλησπόντιος*, *Νησιωτικός*, and *Ἰωνικὸς φόρος*—and thinks this passage should be used as evidence for the early history of the Delian League. It seems more likely that both Aeschylus and the compilers of the treaty lists found it natural to follow some of the more obvious geographical groupings of the islands and the Ionian and Thracian coast.

to west, beginning with Colchis, and ending with the Pillars of Heracles; [41] unless we believe with Wilamowitz that lines 425–35 are an interpolation.[42]

41. The apparent conflict between the order of places here and in Io's journey (*PV* 107–35) would seem to imply that the list of mourning nations is not given in geographical order. But I think it can be shown that the conflict *is* only apparent, and there is no real inconsistency between the two passages. The mourning nations named by the chorus from east to west are the inhabitants of Asia, the warlike maids of Colchis (i.e., Amazons), the Scythians of Lake Maiotis, the "Arabians" of Caucasus, and, if the last two stanzas are genuine, Mt. Atlas, Ocean, and the depths of Hades. Travelling from west to east, Io visits nomad Scyths, Chalybes, Caucasus, Amazons, Maiotis, Asia. Caucasus, Maiotis, and Asia come in inverse order, as they should if both lists are in geographical order. But while the Scyths of the first passage are near Lake Maiotis, those of the second speech seem to be in the far west; and the Amazons of Colchis, by Aeschylean geography, must be a long way from the Amazons near Caucasus. If both passages are in geographical order then they must refer to different Scyths and different Amazons, and this indeed seems to be the case. The Amazons of Colchis and the Scyths of Lake Maiotis need not be the same as the more western Amazons and the nomad Scyths of Io's journey. Herodotus too (4.110–17) locates the Amazons in more than one place, and tells of many different tribes of Scythians between the Danube and the Tanais (4.18–20). Though he does not agree in detail with Aeschylus, he agrees on the main point of locating different branches of these peoples far apart from each other. The location of Ἀραβία near Caucasus in the west is an unsolved difficulty which has caused most editors to assume a corruption, e.g., Wilamowitz, *Aischylos Interpretationen* (Berlin, 1914), p. 155; Paley, in his edition of Aeschylus (*Tragedies of Aeschylus* [London, 1855], ad loc.).

42. *Aischylos*, p. 161.

It is sometimes said that Aeschylus' geographical ideas are careless, confused, or even self-contradictory. Generally speaking this is not true. His information, if not always scientifically accurate, is the result of a serious attempt to inform himself. Havelock has shown that one of the most bewildering passages, the second half of Io's journey, is not the chaotic fantasy it seems to be, but is based on a scientifically thought out geographical system.[43] Aeschylus has visualized this part of her journey quite as clearly as the part through more familiar territory. It is true that as he approaches the edges of the world his geography, both in this passage and in many others, grows more fabulous. But he does not abandon his map. In these distant places are encircling Ocean (*PV* 138–40, 300–2, 531), the Pillars of Heracles and the gardens of the Hesperides (*PV* 348–50, 428–30; fr. 312 inc.), the places of the sun's

43. E. A. Havelock, *The Crucifixion of Intellectual Man* (Boston, 1951), pp. 59–63. Not all the details of Havelock's analysis seem right, e.g., he asserts that Aeschylus regards the Cimmerian Bosporus as the boundary between Asia and Europe (see below, pp. 50–3 for Aeschylus' probable views on this subject). But his main point is convincing, that Io's survey of half the earth is based on the world map of the Ionian geographers, and that Io's journey and that of Heracles in *PL* have, among others, the function of presenting a systematic view of the two halves of the cosmos in this drama of cosmic forces. Io's "route would be recognized by a Hellenic audience as a product of the same science of which Prometheus had earlier been the exponent. . . . She is manipulated to dramatize a theory, one might say, of latitude and longitude . . . the Wanderer, like Prometheus, is a representative of the activities of intellectual man" (pp. 61–2).

rising and setting to which Heracles journeys in a cup (fr. 69 *Heliades;* fr. 192 *PL;* fr. 74 *Heracleidae*), the Hyperboreans (fr. 197 *PL; Cho.* 373), the sinless Gabii who do not know what work is (fr. 196 *PL*), the Rhipaean Mountains (fr. 197 *PL;* fr. 68 *Heliades*), the Graeae, the Arimaspians, the Gorgons, Pluto's ford, the river Aithiops (*PV* 793–809), the Cynocephali (fr. 431 inc.), and the Sternophthalmi (fr. 441 inc.). We may perhaps prefer not to call these geography, but they fit into a clearly conceived scheme of the world. For instance, the Hyperboreans and the Rhipaean Mountains are not just "somewhere" in the north, they are the place where the Ister rises (fr. 197 *PL*), Eridanus is in Spain (fr. 73 *Heliades*), Helius bathes himself and his weary horses in the warm streams of the Arabian Gulf (fr. 192 *PL*).

> φοινικόπεδόν τ' ἐρυθρᾶς ἱερὸν
> χεῦμα θαλάσσης,
> χαλκοκέραυνόν τε παρ' Ὠκεανῷ
> λίμναν παντοτρόφον Αἰθιόπων
> ἵν' ὁ παντόπτας Ἥλιος . . .

But fabulous places are only a small part of Aeschylus' geography.

When Aeschylus' treatment of real places is in question, his statements about the boundaries of Europe and Asia are sometimes used as examples of his careless and inconsistent geography. Apparently he names three boundaries. One, the Thracian Bosporus (*Supp.* 543–7), is recognized everywhere in Greek literature.

He names another boundary at the Phasis river in Colchis (fr. 191 *PL*),

> πῇ μὲν δίδυμον χθονὸς Εὐρώπης
> μέγαν ἠδ' Ἀσίας τέρμονα Φᾶσιν.

In *Prometheus Bound*, according to the usual interpretation, he places it at the Tanais and Cimmerian Bosporus (*PV* 733–4).[44] Herodotus (4.45) also names

44. Greenwood (*Geographical Allusion in Attic Tragedy*, p. 63) regards the whole of Io's journey as fantasy rather than geography, and suggests (n. 3) that Aeschylus "may have thought that the Cimmerian Bosporus was at the mouth of the Phasis." This last is essentially Wilamowitz' solution. In order to save Aeschylus from inconsistency he would have him believe that Phasis and Tanais are two names for the same stream (*Aischylos*, pp. 153 and 157). This, according to him, also explains why Aeschylus calls it a *double* boundary (δίδυμον . . . τέρμονα, fr. 191 *PL*). I prefer the less violent solution proposed by me on p. 52–3. Wilhelm Schmid overlooks this opportunity to reinforce his theory that the *Prometheus* which we have is not the one Aeschylus wrote. If *PV* and *PL* disagree about the boundaries of Europe and Asia it is unlikely that Aeschylus wrote both of them. Schmid, however, while maintaining (*Untersuchungen zum gefesselten Prometheus* in Tübinger Beiträge zur Altertumswissenschaft, *9* [Stuttgart, 1929], 58) that the fantastic element in Io's journey is not typical of Aeschylus, and contrasting it with the more "realistic" journey in *Suppliants*, apparently accepts Wilamowitz' explanation of the Phasis-Tanais problem (p. 97, n. 1). The tradition of the scholiast on *Pers.* 10 (quoted in *TGF*, p. 66) Αἰσχύλος δὲ ἐν Προμηθεῖ λυομένῳ καὶ Σοφοκλῆς ἐν Σκύθαις ὑπὸ τούτου [Tanais] διορίζεσθαί φησι τὰς ἠπείρους, seems to support the idea that Aeschylus confused Phasis and Tanais throughout the Prometheus trilogy. I prefer to think that the mistake is the scholiast's. Sophocles' views on this question are discussed below, p. 98.

Phasis as the boundary of Europe and Asia, but adds that others make the boundary Τάναϊν πόταμον τὸν Μαιήτην καὶ Πορθμήια τὰ Κιμμέρια. But the fact that others make Tanais the boundary is no proof that Aeschylus did. If, in two plays of the same trilogy, Aeschylus can contradict himself about the boundaries of Europe and Asia, his geography can scarcely be called definite or systematic. However, another interpretation of the text of the Tanais passage is possible. Prometheus is describing Io's eastward journey to her (*PV* 729–35)—

> ἰσθμὸν δ' ἐπ' αὐταῖς στενοπόροις λίμνης πύλαις
> Κιμμερικὸν ἥξεις, ὃν θρασυσπλάγχνως σε χρὴ
> λιποῦσαν αὐλῶν' ἐκπερᾶν Μαιωτικόν·
> ἔσται δὲ θνητοῖς εἰσαεὶ λόγος μέγας
> τῆς σῆς πορείας, Βόσπορος δ' ἐπώνυμος
> κεκλήσεται. λιποῦσα δ' Εὐρώπης πέδον
> ἤπειρον ἥξεις 'Ασιάδα.

Greek does not require that the last sentence refer to the crossing of the Cimmerian Bosporus. The δέ and the future ἥξεις rather separate the crossing into Asia from what goes before. In lines 729–30 the same words (δέ . . . ἥξεις) definitely introduce a new stage of the journey. Lines 790–2 support this interpretation. Taking up his interrupted prophecy Prometheus continues,

> ὅταν περάσῃς ῥεῖθρον ἠπείροιν ὅρον,
> πρὸς ἀντολὰς φλογῶπας ἡλίου στίβει
> πόντου παρεῖσα φλοῖσβον.

According to Liddell and Scott there is no case of *ῥεῖθρον* meaning anything but river. To translate it "strait," as we must if it refers to the Cimmerian Bosporus, is, while not impossible, stretching it beyond its natural meaning. The simplest interpretation of the Greek is that the *ῥεῖθρον* is the River Phasis, near the end of the Black Sea. In that case *παρεῖσα* means "leaving aside." Travelling eastward, Io leaves the shores of the Black Sea behind her. If this is correct there is no contradiction. Aeschylus, like Herodotus, visualizes the continent of Asia as bounded by the Thracian Bosporus and the River Phasis. The confusion has been read into Aeschylus, who, as usual, has a clear picture of his geography.

Undoubtedly Aeschylus sometimes makes mistakes, but many of his so-called "mistakes" can be explained away—like the Phasis-Tanais confusion. For example, he seems to put Salmydessus on the Asiatic rather than the Thracian coast of the Black Sea (*PV* 724–7);[45] and Strabo (12.580) says that he mixes everything up (*συγχεῖ*) in his description of the kingdom of Tantalus, apparently because he regards Mount Ida and Mount Sipylus as part of the same kingdom (fr. 158, 162, 163 *Niobe*). In the first case he is speaking of the Amazons

> *αἳ Θεμίσκυράν ποτε*
> *κατοικιοῦσιν ἀμφὶ Θερμώδονθ', ἵνα*
> *τραχεῖα πόντου Σαλμυδησσία γνάθος*
> *ἐχθρόξενος ναύταισι, μητρυιὰ νεῶν.*

45. See Wilamowitz, *Aischylos*, p. 157.

If the Salmydessian jaws are the Symplegades rather than the city, it is not very farfetched, though less precise than his usual style, to describe them as in the neighborhood of Themiscyra and Thermodon, since the Symplegades lay between the Asian and Thracian coasts of Pontus. As for the kingdom of Tantalus, it seems likely that he is thinking of an immensely extended prehistoric realm that includes both Lydia and the Troad, just as Pelasgus' realm in *Suppliants* includes all of mainland Greece to the Strymon.

Aeschylus' information about better known parts of the world is often accurate and complete, and he represents distant places in vivid and concrete detail.

About Egypt and the Nile Aeschylus has much lore. It is the three-cornered Nile land, where the descendants of Io will found Naucratis (*PV* 814–15), bordering on Syria (*Supp.* 5), a land made by the Nile (*PV* 852), the site of Thebes (*Pers.* 38) and Memphis (*Pers.* 36; *Supp.* 310). He mentions the marsh dwellers (*Pers.* 39) *ἑλειοβάται ναῶν ἐρέται* (cf. Hdt. 2.92–5), and the national food and drink, byblus fruit and barley beer (*Supp.* 761 and 953). Of the Nile itself he mentions the lifegiving fertilizing waters (*Supp.* 855–7), its healing qualities (*Supp.* 561), its seven (fr. 300 inc.) sandy (*Supp.* 3–4) mouths, the delta (*πρόσχωμα*) and the Canopic mouth (*PV* 846–7), its source in the Byblus mountains (*PV* 811–12). This probably refers not to the Syrian Byblus, but to the mountains of southern Egypt to which the byblus, or papyrus, is native.[46] If so this is another case of rather extraordi-

46. PW, *3*, 1099, s.v. *byblos.*

nary accuracy. The cause of the flooding of the Nile he rightly attributes to melting snows (*Supp.* 558–61; fr. 300 inc.).[47] One of the passages describing this phenomenon is characteristic of the concreteness and vividness of his geographical descriptions (fr. 300 inc.).

> *γένος μὲν αἰνεῖν ἐκμαθὼν ἐπίσταμαι*
> *Αἰθιοπίδος γῆς, ἔνθα Νεῖλος ἑπτάρους*
> *γαῖαν κυλίνδων πνευμάτων ἐπομβρίᾳ,*
> *ἐν ᾗ πυρωτὸν φέγγος ἐκλάμψαν φλόγα*
> *τήκει πετραίαν χιόνα· πᾶσα δ' εὐθαλὴς*
> *Αἴγυπτος ἁγνοῦ νάματος πληρουμένη*
> *φερέσβιον Δήμητρος ἀντέλλει στάχυν.*

It is not only the accuracy of his information but the definiteness and brilliance of his language that gives such a satisfying feeling of reality to Aeschylus' geographical descriptions.

He gives us fewer facts about Asia but here too his statements have the definiteness of verified knowledge. I have already discussed his view of the boundaries of that continent. The phrase *πολυάνδρου δ' Ἀσίας* (*Pers.* 73) suggests that the Greeks, like modern Europeans, were impressed by the teeming populations of Asia. He speaks of cities subject to Persia (*Pers.* 875–7),

> *Ἕλλας τ' ἀμφὶ πόρον πλατὺν εὐχόμεναι, μυχία τε*
> *προποντίς,*
> *καὶ στόμωμα πόντου.*

47. According to Kranz (*Stasimon*, p. 101) he is the first known Greek to suggest the correct explanation.

Hellespont, the recessed Sea of Marmora, and the Bosporus opening on the Black Sea are given in order, and in each case a single word gives the essential visual quality of the place—πλατύν, μυχία, στόμωμα. Even a passing reference can make a picture with clearly defined spatial relationships. The passages on the Cimmerian Bosporus and the Symplegades (*PV* 723–30) have some of the same qualities. The precision of the passage just quoted makes it seem unlikely that earlier in *Persae* Aeschylus confuses Hellespont and Bosporus (*Pers.* 722–3). I believe that in this earlier passage Aeschylus uses Bosporus loosely of the whole waterway from the Black Sea to the Aegean, as Sophocles also seems to do (*Ajax* 884; fr. 462 *Poimenes*).

A passage in *Persae* (*Pers.* 867, already discussed in another context above, p. 47 with n. 40) contains an out of the way bit of lore. He speaks of cities subject to Darius

> οἷαι Στρυμονίου πελάγους Ἀχελωίδες εἰσὶ πάροικοι
> Θρηΐκων ἐπαύλεις.

The "watery steadings of the Strymonian sea [i.e., Lake Prasias] which are neighbors of the Thracians," are probably the pile houses of Lake Prasias described by Herodotus (5.16).[48] It is unlikely that the ἐπαύλεις

48. ἐπαύλεις is Wilamowitz' emendation for ἐπαύλων. Murray follows him in the O.C.T. The reference to pile dwellings is not altered by retaining the original text, though the sentence becomes slightly more complicated, i.e., "such watery cities [πόλεις is the antecedent] of the Strymonian sea as are neighbors of the Thracian steadings."

Ἀχελωίδες are islands at the mouth of the Strymon off the coast of Thrace. Two separate stanzas are devoted to the islands, and Lemnos, which *is* off the coast of Thrace, is mentioned there. Furthermore, the following line,

λίμνας τ' ἔκτοθεν αἳ κατὰ χέρσον ἐληλαμέναι . . .

calls attention to the λίμνη—which is properly a lake, though in poetry it is used of the sea often enough—and makes a distinction between the cities in it and those outside it (ἔκτοθεν), i.e., on dry land. If he is speaking of islands the language is redundant, and he has passed over with scarcely a mention the group of cities on the Thracian coast where Megabazos and Mardonius campaigned while Darius sat on the other side of the Halys (Hdt. 5.11–17 and 6.44–8).[49] If he is referring to the pile dwellings of Lake Prasias he is following his usual procedure, taking the cities of the coast in geographical order from the Strymon to the Bosporus, and then taking the islands by groups.[50]

The description of the eruption of Aetna is another passage of peculiar vividness and brilliance—so much so that most scholars assume that it must have been written after the poet had seen Aetna in action, and

49. According to Herodotus 5.16, however, Megabazos never succeeded in conquering the lake dwellers.

50. This interpretation was apparently first suggested in 1852 by H. Weil, in his edition of Aeschylus (*Tragoediae* [Leipzig, 1852]). His terse note ad loc. seems to me to take care of all objections.

date the play accordingly.[51] As usual it is precision of detail that has given the impression Aeschylus is describing something he has seen himself (*PV* 363–72).

> *καὶ νῦν ἀχρεῖον καὶ παράορον δέμας*
> *κεῖται στενωποῦ πλησίον θαλασσίου*
> *ἰπούμενος ῥίζαισιν Αἰτναίαις ὕπο.*
> *κορυφαῖς δ' ἐν ἄκραις ἥμενος μυδροκτυπεῖ*
> *Ἥφαιστος, ἔνθεν ἐκραγήσονταί ποτε*
> *ποταμοὶ πυρὸς δάπτοντες ἀγρίαις γνάθοις*
> *τῆς καλλικάρπου Σικελίας λευροὺς γύας·*
> *τοιόνδε Τυφὼς ἐξαναζέσει χόλον*
> *θερμοῖς ἀπλάτου βέλεσι πυρπνόου ζάλης,*
> *καίπερ κεραυνῷ Ζηνὸς ἠνθρακωμένος.*

The dazzling reality of the scene comes from concrete details—the strait, the rivers of fire feeding on the smooth acres of Sicily, the boiling up of *χόλος*, the unapproachable fiery foam.

A few lesser geographical observations should be mentioned. Rhegium got its name *ὥς φησὶν Αἰσχύλος, διὰ τὸ συμβὰν πάθος τῇ χώρᾳ ταύτῃ· ἀπορραγῆναι γὰρ ἀπὸ τῆς ἠπείρου τὴν Σικελίαν ὑπὸ σεισμῶν* . . . (fr. 402 inc. = Strabo 6.258)—a curious little piece of in-

51. E.g., Wilamowitz, *Aischylos*, p. 121. So strongly does this passage indicate a date in the neighborhood of 475 B.C. that W. Schmid (*Untersuchungen zum gefesselten Prometheus*, pp. 5–15) finds it necessary to treat the whole Oceanus scene as an interpolation in order to save his theory of a late 5th century date for *PV*. The eyewitness may have been Pindar, whose description of Aetna erupting (*Pythian* 1.19–28) could have inspired this passage.

formation with a Herodotean flavor. The story of Heracles among the Ligurians (fr. 199 *PL*) shows that he knew about the stony area described by Strabo (4.183).

Aeschylus' interest is mainly in topography and peoples. Of natural products he mentions only the byblus and barley beer. And only two strange animals appear.[52] We find the *βούβαλις*, or African antelope (fr. 330 inc.), also mentioned by Herodotus (4.192), and the labors of the Aetnaean beetle (fr. 233 *Sisyphus*). No doubt Sisyphus was compared to the beetle with his ball of dung.[53]

Aeschylus' description of foreign places, whether real or fabulous, all show the same qualities. The details which give them their vividness are not inventions of the imagination, but facts, or what Aeschylus took for facts. He represents the remote and the exotic with as much precision as the knowledge of his day will permit.

Distribution

Most of Aeschylus' foreign references come from *Suppliants* and *Persae*. *Prometheus* has fewer, though it contributes some of the most interesting geographical passages. If *Seven* and *Oresteia* had survived without the other three plays Aeschylus would not have

52. I exclude fabulous creations like Oceanus' bird and the τραγέλαφος mocked by Aristophanes (*Frogs* 935).

53. Cf. Aristophanes *Peace* 73, and schol. ad loc.

acquired the reputation of a poet interested in foreign peoples and places.

In the fragments too the foreign references are limited to a small group of plays. Except for *Sisyphus*, *Heracleidae*, and "incerta," all the lost plays with foreign references also have obviously foreign subject matter—*Edoni*, *Lycurgus*, *Niobe*, *Aetnaeae*, *Heliades*, and *Prometheus Unbound*, which, of all the lost plays, is the most quoted with reference to foreign matters. *Cares*, *Mysi*, and *Glaucus* add some interesting foreign place names, though none of their surviving fragments contains any actual information.

The distribution of names of foreign places and peoples in the plays and fragments also suggests that foreign material is confined to a small group of plays with primarily foreign subjects. While not in itself conclusive, it can furnish a usable key to the distribution of foreign material. Counting passages to demonstrate this only leads to confusion, since a "passage" can be anything from one word to several hundred lines, and there is no way of setting up a workable standard. Not counting repetitions, 89 of the 100 names of foreign peoples and places occur in *Suppliants*, *Persae*, and *Prometheus*. *Seven* and *Oresteia* together contain only 29, the fragments 39. *Seven*, laid in Greece, with no foreign characters, contains only two foreign place names; *Agamemnon*, with Cassandra and its background of the Trojan war, has nine; *Choephoroe*, with its chorus of captive barbarians, and *Eumenides* have nine each (see Appendix). All this indicates a rather obvious point, but one not sufficiently stressed in discussions of Aeschylus as an "orientalizing" poet in love with his barbaric effects[54]—namely, this great richness of foreign information is confined to a few plays with foreign subject matter. *Seven* has less foreign material than any extant play of that "purely Greek" poet, Sophocles. In fact, it has only the references to Chalybian and Scythian iron (*Sept.* 727–8 and 818). The fragments too are much less rich in foreign material than those of Sophocles (see below, pp. 64–114), and we have seen that practically all of it comes from plays with recognizably foreign subject matter. Which points again toward the same conclusion—that in general Aeschylus did not concern himself with foreign material, but tried to represent foreigners accurately and completely in the plays in which they occur. It is an accident that three of the seven surviving plays are so rich in foreign material that we have come to think of Aeschylus as a poet greatly preoccupied with barbarians.

54. E.g., Kranz, *Stasimon*, p. 72, "Gerade dieses Wunderbare des Orientalischen, des Ausserhellenischen überhaupt, dessen Reiz und Wirkung ebenso im Phantastischen wie im Wissenswerten liegen kann, ist in der Tat ein echtes Element des archaischen und reifarchaischen Spieles." And p. 108, "Hellenisches und Ausserhellenisches ist ganz und gar durcheinandergewirkt zu einer neuen, künstlerischen Einheit, in der aber beide Elemente ihr Gewicht haben, einer der Wesenszüge der archaischen und reifarchaischen Kunst."

Conclusion

In fact, if my suggestions are correct, Aeschylus' handling of foreign material is the reverse of orientalizing. The orientalizing style introduces "oriental" motifs for their own sake, regardless of subject matter, to fill and decorate spaces. We have seen that Aeschylus does have some formulaic foreign references, but even these are not always used in this manner. By far the greater number of foreign references occur only where the context demands them. Far from being introduced for decorative purposes, they are essential parts of the story. As I have shown, there is no question of an occasional exotic touch to add variety and interest. A foreign character in Aeschylus is consistently foreign. Foreignness is part of the characterization, and the poet constantly reminds us of it. He builds and maintains a foreign atmosphere by repeated references to speech and dress and manners, to foreign legends and distant places. And there is no vagueness in his foreign representations, but almost always the concrete individual detail. He represents not "the barbarian" of tradition, but *a* Persian, *a* Trojan, *an* Egyptian, and he has clear notions about their differences in language, dress, customs, and appearance, beliefs. His foreign landscapes are not just distant and exotic scenes, but places on a map, with precise, and sometimes accurate, climate and topography.

Aeschylus differentiates among barbarian peoples, and bases his differentiation on detailed information.

This takes the emphasis off foreignness as such, and the related idea of the superiority of Greeks to all foreigners. We have seen in fact that this is not an important theme in Aeschylus. For the moment it is enough to point out that it is difficult to maintain the Greek-barbarian antithesis when there is no "barbarian" as such, but instead many different and fascinating varieties of human beings.

3. SOPHOCLES

Language

Only one reference to the fact that a character speaks a foreign language exists in the extant plays of Sophocles (*Ajax* 1263). None has survived in the fragments. Tecmessa's foreignness might, like Cassandra's in *Agamemnon*, have been developed by drawing attention to her speech, but Sophocles does not raise the point. There are two passing general references to foreign speech. Heracles (*Trach.* 1060) in describing his suffering cries out that "neither Greece nor any tongueless land" (οὔθ' Ἑλλάς, οὔτ' ἄγλωσσος) ever did such a thing to him as Dejaneira has done. Ἄγλωσσος is simply a way of expressing the basic idea in the word βάρβαρος, that a foreign language is a set of meaningless sounds. In *Antigone* (1001–2) Teiresias refers to the fact that the omens have become unintelligible by saying the birds spoke an unknown (unintelligible?) foreign language.

> ἀγνῶτ' ἀκούω φθόγγον ὀρνίθων, κακῷ
> κλάζοντας οἴστρῳ καὶ βεβαρβαρωμένῳ.

But Sophocles was evidently aware of the dramatic possibilities of dialect, and exploited them in some of the lost plays. The scholiast on Euripides' *Phoenissae* 301 compares the foreign accent of the chorus to that of a character in Sophocles' lost play, *Helenes Apaitesis*, and quotes the following passage in illustration (fr. 178):[1]

> *καὶ γὰρ χαρακτὴρ αὐτὸς ἐν γλώσσῃ τί με*
> *παρηγορεῖ Λάκωνος ὀσμᾶσθαι λόγου.*

If he used Laconian dialect it is not unlikely that he also used foreign pronunciation as a dramatic device. The evidence of the fragments indicates that this was in fact the case. Ἴαννα occurs three times in the fragments (fr. 53 *Aechmalotides;* fr. 476 *Poimenes;* fr. 560 *Triptolemus*). Hesychius implies that Sophocles uses the word as Aeschylus does, to give a foreign accent, as it were, to some non-Greek character (see above, p. 18 with n. 5).[2] Since the three plays in which it occurs all involve foreigners, we may be fairly sure that this is the case. Γραῖκες (fr. 475 *Poimenes*), and the alternative form Ῥαικοί (fr. 983 inc.), which have furnished

1. J. Rasch (*Sophocles quid debeat Herodoto in rebus ad fabulas exornandas adhibitis,* Commentationes Philologicae Jenenses, *10* [Leipzig, 1913], 114–15) also uses this passage as evidence that Sophocles portrayed the speech of foreigners realistically in some lost plays. No one, as far as I can discover, has seen the implications of this point. Cf. Aesch., *Cho.* 563–4.

2. See A. C. Pearson, *The Fragments of Sophocles* (3 vols. Cambridge, 1917), note on fr. 56 (= fr. 53 N *Aechmalotides*).

our barbarian name for the Greeks, are also used, probably for the same purpose.[3]

The clearest indication that Sophocles exploited the dramatic possibilities of foreign language is the large number of foreign words he used.[4] We know of 20

3. The genuineness and meaning of these two words is not entirely certain. Stephanus of Byzantium (p. 212, 20, cited in *TGF*, p. 245) says, Γραικός, ὁ Ἕλλην—Γραῖκες δὲ παρὰ Ἀλκμᾶνι αἱ τῶν Ἑλλήνων μητέρες, καὶ παρὰ Σοφοκλεῖ ἐν Ποιμέσιν. And Photius (*Lex.* p. 480, 15, cited in *TGF*, p. 350) explains οἱ βάρβαροι τοὺς Ἕλληνας. Σοφοκλῆς τῇ λέξει κέχρηται. But according to Eustathius (*Il.* p. 890, 14, cited in *TGF*, p. 350) the form without Γ is used only by barbarians, and does not occur in Sophocles. L & S give other examples of Γραικός, s.v. H. Degen (*De Troianis scaenicis* [diss. Leipzig, 1900], p. 38) maintains, with a formidable array of authorities, that Γραῖκες cannot be related to Γραικοί, and whatever Sophocles meant by it—he suggests mothers of the Hellenes, relating it to the root γρα- as in γραῦς—he was not using it as a foreign name for the Greeks. Pearson in his note to fr. 518 (*Fragments of Sophocles* = fr. 475 N *Poimenes*) is skeptical for the same reasons.

4. Foreign words, like the whole subject of foreign material in Sophocles, have received very little attention. Degen (*De Troianis scaenicis*, pp. 38–41), in a discussion of foreign words used in connection with Troy by all three tragedians, lists some of those used by Sophocles. But, since he treats tragic diction as a whole, he has no conclusions about the individual writers. Rasch (*Sophocles quid debeat Herodoto*, pp. 114–16 with notes) discusses the foreign words of the fragments. As far as I can discover, neither Rasch nor anyone else has considered what his discussion implies about Sophocles' style. H. B. Dunkel (*Panhellenism in Greek Tragedy* [diss. Chicago, 1937], p. 23) speaks of "linguistic realism" in *Poimenes*, a good description, but he asserts that βαλλήν (Soph. fr. 472 *Poimenes*) is "the only instance in Attic tragedy

(only two less than Aeschylus, if we exclude the 49 Persian names). All but one of these occur in the fragments. In the extant plays we find σινδών, an oriental word of uncertain provenience which also occurs in Aeschylus (see above, p. 22), used of the rope with which Antigone hanged herself (*Ant.* 1222), apparently without exotic overtones, as a word in common use; and μάγος (a Persian word of Assyrian origin, Boisacq s.v.), an insult which Oedipus hurls at Teiresias when he is accusing him and Creon of conspiracy (*OT* 387). If it is true, as Rasch thinks, that μάγος, beyond its usual meaning "priestly impostor," refers to the conspiracy of the Magian Smerdis (Hdt.

---

of the use of a foreign language as part of the characterization of a speaker or as an attempt at local color." What about *Persae* and *Suppliants*, to say nothing of the other fragments of Sophocles? Krausse (*De Euripide Aeschyli instauratore*, pp. 207–8) has observed the foreign vocabulary of *Poimenes* and *Troilus*. Schmid (Schmid-Stählin, I², 488, n. 1) includes eight foreign words in his list of words with unfamiliar roots. None of these writers regards the foreign words as important enough to call for more than passing comment. The most extensive studies of Sophocles' fragments (Pearson, *Fragments of Sophocles;* Blumenthal in PW; Schmid-Stählin, pp. 422–54; and C. R. Post, *The Dramatic Art of Sophocles as Revealed by the Fragments of the Lost Plays,* Harvard Studies in Classical Philology, *33* [1922], 1 ff) scarcely notice the foreign material in the fragments. F. R. Earp (*The Style of Sophocles* [Cambridge, 1944]) deals only with the extant plays. I have therefore been limited in my study of foreign words in Sophocles to the information in *TGF*, Ellend's *Lexicon Sophocleum,* and Rasch, and such help as I could glean from Boisacq, Frisk, and L & S.

3.61 ff), there is a powerful literary allusion here.[5] Creon is called ὁ πιστός two lines earlier, the name for the intimates of the Great King. This suggests that Sophocles really does intend a comparison between Oedipus' imagined situation and the story in Herodotus.

In the fragments, in addition to σινδών (fr. 210 P *Eurypylus*, quoted below, p. 75), we find the following 18 foreign words:

βαίτη, a tent or cloak of skins (fr. 1031 inc.), a Thracian word (L & S, s.v. According to Frisk, s.v., the derivation is not known; cf. Hdt. 4.64).

βάκκαρις, incense (fr. 929 inc.), a Lydian word, also used by Aeschylus (see above, p. 21).

βαλλήν, lord (fr. 472 *Poimenes*, also used by Aeschylus, see p. 20 above).

βαρίβας, a sailor, or man who goes on a βᾶρις (fr. 474 *Poimenes;* on Aeschylus' use of βᾶρις see above, p. 20).

ἰαί, called by Hesychius (4.338, quoted in *TGF*, p. 442) a βάρβαρον θρήνημα (fr. 574 *Troilus*).

κάνναβις, hemp (fr. 222 *Thamyras*), a loan word of uncertain origin (Hdt. 4.74–5; Boisacq and Frisk, s.v.).

κινάκης, a sword (fr. 958 inc.), a shortened form of the Persian word for sword (Hdt. 3.118, 128; Boisacq and Frisk, s.v. ἀκινάκης).

5. See Rasch, *Sophocles quid debeat Herodoto*, pp. 106–7.

μάγαδις, a lyre or harp (fr. 217 *Thamyras*), an "Asiatic" word (Boisacq, s.v.).

μαγίς, a cake, or table(?) (fr. 668 inc.), an Egyptian word (Photius, *Bibliotheca*, 553 b 10, quoted in *TGF*, p. 291).

νάβλα, a lyre or harp, if the reading is correct (fr. 765 inc.; see below, p. 76), a Semitic word (Boisacq, s.v.).[6]

ὀρίνδη, a rice cake (fr. 552 *Triptolemus*), a loan word of uncertain origin (Boisacq, s.v.).

ὀροσάγγαι, king's benefactors (fr. 184 *Helenes Gamos;* fr. 577 *Troilus*), a Persian word (Hdt. 8.85).

παρασάγγης (fr. 121 *Andromache;* fr. 477 *Poimenes*). Apparently Sophocles used it to mean "messenger," instead of as a measure of distance, the meaning familiar to the Greeks (*Etymologicum Magnum*, p. 652, 13, quoted in *TGF*, p. 157).

σάρητον, a barbarian tunic (fr. 131 *Andromeda*), the same as the *σάραπις*, which is a Περσικὸς

6. *TGF gives* οὐ νάβλα κωκυτοῖσιν, οὐ λύρα φίλη. Οὐ νάβλα is Brunck's reading for codd. ἐν αὐλᾷ or οὐ ναῦλα. Φίλη is Schneidwin's suggestion for φίλα. Pearson in his note to fr. 849 (= fr. 765 N inc.) rejects these changes for Wagener's ἔναυλα on not very convincing grounds. The desire to get rid of foreign words in Sophocles may come from not recognizing how much he used them.

χιτὼν μεσόλευκος (Hesychius 4.6, 10, 11, quoted in *TGF*, p. 159; see below, pp. 90–2).[7]

σίκλος, a coin (fr. 990 inc.), from a Semitic word meaning "weight," the original of "shekel" (Boisacq, s.v. σίγλος σίκλος).[8]

σισυρνώδης, an adjective from σίσυρνα, a cloak of skin or hide (fr. 379 *Mysi; σίσυρνα* is used by Aeschylus; see above, p. 21).

σκάλμη, a sword (fr. 563 *Troilus*), a barbarian word according to Pollux (10.165, quoted in *TGF*, p. 267).

τιάρα, traditional Persian headdress (fr. 379 *Mysi;* also used by Aeschylus; see above, p. 22).

From the quantity of foreign words in the fragments it is clear that Sophocles made a good deal more of the language of his foreign characters than his treatment of Tecmessa would lead us to expect. We have mentioned that, if we exclude the 49 Persian proper names, we find Aeschylus and Sophocles used almost the same number of foreign words. The location of

7. On the authenticity of the Persian tunic with the white panel see Gow, "Notes on the *Persae*," pp. 148 ff, and Pearson's note to fr. 135 (= fr. 131 N *Andromeda*).

8. Pearson in his note to fr. 1094 (= fr. 990 N inc.) records his doubts, and those of other scholars, that Sophocles ever used this word. They suggest that Photius—our source—really meant to refer to Xenophon, *Anabasis* 1.5, 6, or that Sophocles used the Greek σίγλα or σίγλης, an earring. Is this because they have not noticed how many other genuinely foreign words Sophocles uses?

these words is significant. Eight of Aeschylus' foreign words occur in the fragments, 18 of Sophocles'. These 18 words plus Ἴαννα, Γραῖκες, Ῥαικοί, which are here included as being for dramatic purposes in the same category, are distributed among nine lost plays of Sophocles as follows: *Aechmalotides* 1, *Andromache* 1, *Andromeda* 1, *Helenes Gamos* 1, *Thamyras* 2, *Mysi* 2, *Poimenes* 5, *Triptolemus* 2, *Troilus* 3. Seven others (counting Ῥαικοί, fr. 983 inc.) occur in plays whose titles have been lost. No lost play of Aeschylus has produced more than one foreign word. No extant play of Aeschylus has produced more than seven (*Supp.* has Ἰαόνιος, βᾶρις, βοῦνις, καρβάν, μᾶ, πᾶ, and probably χάμψα).

With the exception of μάγος (*OT* 387) and σινδών (*Ant.* 1222), and six words whose source is uncertain (fr. 668, 765, 929, 958, 990, 1031 inc.), all the foreign words of Sophocles occur in plays with foreign settings, or foreign characters, or both. Apparently, like Aeschylus, he used them as part of a foreign characterization. This is shown by the appropriateness of the context. Persian and Phrygian words, for example, usually occur in plays with settings, in or near the Troad (for the tendency for the tragedians to assimilate the cultural characteristics of Trojan, Phrygian, and Persian see below, pp. 101–4). *Aechmalotides*, *Andromache*, *Mysi*, *Poimenes*, *Troilus*, *Helenes Gamos*, whether laid in the Troad or elsewhere, certainly involved Trojan characters. The appropriateness of κάνναβις and μάγαδις to the Thracian Thamyras is obvious. It is unthinkable that all these outlandish words should have occurred only as literary allusions like μάγος in *Oedipus*. Clearly, in some of the lost plays, there were characters whose speech was as foreign as the Danaids'.

Like Aeschylus, Sophocles used foreign words in dialogue as well as in lyric passages. Τιάρα, σίσυρα, σκάλμη, μάγαδις, νάβλα, and probably ὀρίνδη, all occur in lines of iambic trimeter. They are not then only for lyric decoration, but are used to convey information and, in some cases, to characterize the speech of foreigners. For example, σκάλμη is used by a Trojan eunuch (see below, p. 80).

This evidence throws some doubt on the view which contrasts a purely "Greek" Sophocles with an "orientalizing" Aeschylus.[9] Sophocles' foreign vocabu-

9. E.g., Kranz, *Stasimon*, p. 108. "Es ist die klare Grenzlinie zwischen der vorklassischen und der klassischen bildenden Kunst Athens, dass diese alles aus ihrem Bereich weist, was nicht dem hellenischen Menschen schlechthin zu Erscheinung und Sein verhilft. . . . Das gleiche Gesetz gilt von der klassischen Wortkunst. Auch ihr ewiges Thema ist; der hellenische Mensch als Mensch schlechthin." He ignores all the lost plays involving foreign material except *Triptolemus*, which he dismisses as an uncharacteristic "Jugendwerk," written under the influence of Aeschylus. This is the usual explanation for any foreign material from the fragments that has been noticed. Paul Friedländer (*Die griechische Tragödie und das Tragische*, Part 3 ["Die Antike," *2* (1926)], 104) characterizes the three tragedians as follows: "Bei Aischylus war das Unhellenische—der Ägypterherold in den 'Schutzflehenden,' die 'Perser'—gleichsam Rest eines noch kaum überwundenen Zustandes, da Athen sich eben erst aus

lary is as extensive and as curious as Aeschylus'. By an accident no play of Sophocles has survived which uses this vocabulary. It is also an accident that has preserved for us *Persae*, *Suppliants*, and *Agamemnon*, with their concentration on foreign speech. The fragments suggest that, at least in the matter of language, Aeschylus' and Sophocles' treatment of foreigners had more in common than is usually thought.

Physical appearance

Sophocles refers only once to the different physical appearance of foreign peoples (fr. 363 *Manteis*),

ἔπειτα γῆρας λαμβάνει σφ' Αἰγύπτιον.

This is the riddle of the mulberry which is first white, then red, then black. He compares its final complexion to that of the Egyptians. This almost complete lack of material does not prove that Sophocles never

---

der Umarmung des Orients befreite. Bei Sophocles fehlt das 'barbarische' Element vollkommen—ganz ebenso wie am plastischen Schmuck des Parthenon. Euripides hingegen hat sich gern der bunten Fremdheit bedient." See also Cedric Whitman, *Sophocles, a Study in Heroic Humanism* (Cambridge, 1951), p. 44. The question whether realistic presentation of foreigners is characteristic of an early "Aeschylean" period is discussed below, pp. 104–111. Only Wilamowitz (*Einleitung in die Attische Tragödie* [Berlin, 1889], pp. 31–2) shows some awareness—and that is unsubstantiated—of the extent to which Sophocles exploited knowledge of foreign peoples and places afforded by contemporary ἱστορία.

referred to racial differences in the lost plays. If Aeschylus' *Suppliants* had not happened to survive we would have the impression that Aeschylus also paid no attention to this subject.

Costume

Again all the evidence comes from the fragments. The σάρητον (fr. 131 *Andromeda*), or Persian cloak, refers to a specific type of garment, the white and purple tunic worn by the Persian kings (see above, pp. 69–70 with n. 7). It is not just a vague name for any kind of foreign attire. A fragment of *Mysi* (379) describes the dress of one of the characters,

ψαλίδας, τιάρας καὶ σισυρνώδη στολήν.

The τιάρα we have met already (see above, pp. 22 and 70). The unintelligible ψαλίδας has been emended by Berk to ψελία, "bracelets," which are vouched for as part of Persian dress by Herodotus (9.80) and Xenophon (*Cyropaedia* 6.4, 2). The σισυρνώδης στολή must be the Persian cloak which, to the Greeks, looked like the coat or blanket of hide, which country people called by the Thraco-Phrygian name σίσυρα (see above, p. 21 and Aristophanes, *Wasps* 1132 ff.).[10] This is not much, but it is information of a fairly concrete and specific nature.

The leopard skin that hung outside Antenor's door as a signal to the Greeks to spare his house was ap-

10. See Pearson's note to fr. 413 (= fr. 379 N *Mysi*).

parently a kind of vest or jacket (σπολάς, fr. 10 *Aias Lokros*).

καταστίκτου κυνὸς
σπολὰς Λίβυσσα παρδαληφόρον δέρος.

In *Aechmalotides* some luxurious piece of material is called (fr. 42) ἄχνην Λυδῆς κερκίδος, "foam of the Lydian shuttle"—a fine expression for the delicacy of the foreign stuff. In *Eurypylus* the wrappings of the hero's corpse are referred to (fr. 210 P, 67–8),

πολλὴ δὲ σινδὼν πολλὰ δ' Ἰστριανίδων
ὕφη γυναικῶν.

σινδών we have already mentioned (above, p. 67). The cloth of Ister was of very fine quality. Wilamowitz has pointed out that it is an anachronism to mention it in connection with the heroes of Troy, since Ister was a colony of Miletus, founded sometime in the 7th century.[11]

The fragments of Aeschylus contain only three references to foreign dress. We get our impressions of his extensive knowledge from *Suppliants* and *Persae*. As we have seen, the fragments of Sophocles contain five references to foreign dress. Had those nine lost plays of Sophocles, containing so many foreign words, survived they might have yielded equally rich information about foreign appearance and costume.

11. See Pearson's note to fr. 210 (not in *TGF*), and Wilamowitz, "Die Spürhunde des Sophokles," *Neue Jahrbücher für das klassische Altertum Geschichte und deutsche Literatur*, 29 (1912), 451.

Objects

The extant plays have nothing of importance. The anachronistic Tyrrhenian trumpet (see above, p. 32) is mentioned in *Ajax* 17. There is a passing reference to the Barcaean chariots of the contestants from Cyrene at the Pythian games (*El.* 727). But the fragments provide a rich collection.

There are five foreign musical instruments. Μάγαδις (fr. 217 *Thamyras*), πηκτίς (fr. 220 *Thamyras;* fr. 378 *Mysi*), τρίγωνος (fr. 218 *Thamyras;* fr. 378 *Mysi*) are all Asiatic types of harp, capable of more complex music than the lyre and cithara. It is not known exactly how they differed from each other.[12] We can assume that all three were polyphonic, since Plato banishes the τρίγωνος and πηκτίς from his ideal state, and all other instruments ὅσα πολύχορδα καὶ πολυαρμονία (*Republic* 399c), and Aristoxenus (635e) discusses πηκτίς and μάγαδις together as types of doublestringed harp. The νάβλα (fr. 765 inc.), if Sophocles really used the word, was a Semitic instrument of the same type.[13] The ἔλυμος (fr. 412 *Niobe;* fr. 586 *Tympanistae*) is a double flute, one of whose pipes is bent into the shape of a horn, used in the worship of the Phrygian mother.[14] These are not just vaguely exotic instru-

12. See Pearson note to fr. 412 (= fr. 378 N *Mysi*), and fr. 238 (= 217 N *Thamyras*).

13. See Pearson note to fr. 849 (= fr. 765 N inc.).

14. See Pearson note to fr. 450 (= fr. 412 N *Niobe*).

ments, but known types that can be recognized and described by writers like Plato and Aristoxenus. And they occur in appropriate contexts. In the play about the Thracian musician, Thamyras, there is some kind of contrast between the Greek lyre and the three kinds of Asiatic harp (see particularly fr. 217 and 220). Because of the state of the text, and our ignorance of the context, we cannot be more precise than this. But clearly such a contrast is relevant in a play about a Thracian musician. The *πηκτίς* and the *τρίγωνος* recur in a play with a chorus of Mysians (fr. 378 *Mysi*). The Phrygian flute is found in the play about the Lydian queen, Niobe, and in *Tympanistae*, which seems to have had a chorus of worshippers of Dionysus or Cybele.[15]

The *κινάκης*, or short Persian sword (fr. 958 inc.), and the *σίκλος*, or shekel (fr. 990 inc.), apply to specific objects identified with specific nationalities. We do not know what plays they occurred in, but it is a good guess that the man who carried the *κινάκης* was a Trojan (see below, pp. 101–4). It is Trojans who carry shields hung with bells (fr. 775 inc.; see above, p. 32 with n. 15). The Scythian *χειρόμακτρα*, made of enemy scalps, which Herodotus describes (4.64), are mentioned in *Oenomaus* (fr. 432),

> *Σκυθιστὶ χειρόμακτρον ἐκδεδαρμένος* (codd. *ἐκκεκαρμένος*).

15. Pearson, *2*, 262–3.

The context of this play is not foreign. But the information in the reference, however it was fitted into the play, could hardly be more precise.[16]

Sophocles' fragments provide more information about objects of foreign use than all the foreign plays of Aeschylus put together. So much precise detail is further evidence that Sophocles in some of the lost plays elaborated the foreign background.

Religion, customs, manners

The almost direct quotation from Herodotus (2.35) about Egyptian customs which are the opposite of Greek customs (*OC* 337–41) suggests a careful use of literary sources. Like *μάγος* (*OT* 387), it is not only mechanically appropriate, but powerfully allusive. But Oedipus' words evoke not so much Herodotus' dispassionate *τὰ πολλὰ πάντα ἔμπαλιν τοῖσι ἄλλοισι ἀνθρώποισι ἐστήσαντο ἤθεά τε καὶ νόμους*, as the disgust of a less experienced Greek reading about manly women

16. We may ask ourselves who does the scalping in a play laid at Pisa in Elis. The answer seems to be Oenomaus, since we know from another source that Sophocles had him roof his palace, or temple, with the skulls of Hippodameia's unsuccessful suitors (schol. Pindar, *Isthmian*, 3.92 [4.54]. See also Pearson's note to fr. 473 = fr. 432 N *Oenomaus*). If so, in spite of the scientific nature of the information, fantasy has here replaced realism. The practice of a real barbarian tribe has been attributed to a mythological Greek king in order to dramatize his savagery.

and womanly men. Such behavior would seem less opposite than inverted. Like μάγος, the reference is introduced as an illustration, in a context which does not involve foreigners in any way, and therefore tells us little about the way in which Sophocles developed foreign subjects. Other references in the extant plays are brief and uninformative. There is a prayer to Ge (*Phil.* 391–403), in which she is represented as the Lydian mother with her lion chariot. What is important here is not her foreignness, but the association of the mountain-going mother with the state of wildness to which Philoctetes has been reduced. There is a reference (*Ajax* 698–700) to the Mysian and Cnossian dances of Pan. Menelaus insists on the "inferiority" of barbarians in his quarrel with Teucer (*Ajax* 1257–63, 1289–1303), but foreignness is not an important theme in the play.

The fragments, on the other hand, are full of detailed information about foreign custom. Since most of the references come from plays with foreign subjects, we may be fairly sure that most of this material was introduced not as interesting digressions, like the reference to the backward customs of the Egyptians, but as necessary parts of the setting or the characterization.

Whether or not Sophocles knew Herodotus as a friend, or read his works, it is clear that he was interested in the same kinds of ethnological material, and learned about them, if not from Herodotus himself, then from some of Herodotus' masters or imitators.[17] I have already quoted the reference to the Scythian χειρόμακτρον—Herodotus' own word for it —in *Oenomaus* (see above, p. 77). In *Phineus* (fr. 646) we find an Egyptian mummy,

νεκρός, τάριχος εἰσορᾶν Αἰγύπτιος.

Compare Herodotus' ταρίχευσις and ταριχεύω in his description of the process of mummification (2.86–90).[18] *Troilus* (fr. 563) refers to the making of a eunuch for the service of the Trojan queen,

σκάλμῃ γὰρ ὄρχεις βασιλὶς ἐκτέμνουσ' ἐμούς.

Compare Herodotus (3.48 and 8.104–6) on the slave trade in boys to be made into eunuchs for the service of the Persian nobility.[19] *Momos* (fr. 390) refers to circumcision, another subject discussed with some interest by Herodotus (2.36–7 and 104). Almost nothing is known about the play except that it appears, on the basis of vocabulary, to have been a satyr play. It is tantalizing not to know whether Sophocles mentioned this practice in connection with one of the peoples to whom Herodotus attributes it (Egyptians, Ethiopians,

17. The most important work on the relation of Sophocles to Herodotus is, of course, Rasch, *Sophocles quid debeat Herodoto.* It is an indispensable collection of parallels, but contains very little analysis of the dramatic uses to which Sophocles puts the Herodotean material.

18. See Pearson note to fr. 712 (= fr. 646 N *Phineus*).

19. The parallel is observed by Rasch, *Sophocles quid debeat Herodoto*, p. 115, n. 2.

Phoenicians, Syrians, Colchians).[20] Herodotus (5.58) says the Ionians call letters Φοινικήια because the Greeks learned them from Cadmus; and in *Poimenes* (fr. 471) we find Sophocles using the phrase Φοινικίοις γράμμασι.[21] We owe this information to Hesychius (4.251, quoted in *TGF*, p. 244), who adds Σοφοκλῆς Ποιμέσιν. ἐπεὶ δοκεῖ Κάδμος αὐτὰ ἐκ Φοινίκης κεκομικέναι. This suggests, though it does not prove, that Sophocles, like Herodotus, attributed the origin of the alphabet to Cadmus.

There are other references of the same variety, but lacking any demonstrable relation to Herodotus; for example, the practice of eating rice and drinking beer (fr. 552 and 553 *Triptolemus*), human sacrifice in Ethiopia (fr. 122 *Andromeda*),[22] sun worship in

20. See Pearson, *2*, 77, and his note to fr. 423 (= fr. 390 N *Momos*).

21. Or we may assume an even closer parallel with Herodotus and punctuate thus with Rasch: φοινικίοις · γράμμασι. In this case the second word, instead of being part of the quotation, is Hesychius' explanation of one of Sophocles' numerous Ionicisms (*Sophocles quid debeat Herodoto*, pp. 108–15). The use of Φοινικήια to mean "letters" in a Teian inscription (IGA 497 B 35 = CIG 3044) of 476–2 B.C. substantiates Herodotus' statement. According to Pearson's note to fr. 514 (= fr. 471 N *Poimenes*) the inscription indicates that the term was prevalent enough so that Sophocles might have picked it up from some other source than Herodotus. But, if we accept the theory of influence at all, it is natural to assume that Ionicisms in Sophocles come from Herodotus. According to Rasch (p. 114) this Ionicism is another bit of the foreign local color so prevalent in *Poimenes*.

22. The text of the fragment is very corrupt. Pearson's

Thrace (fr. 523 *Tereus*).[23] A fragment of an unknown play is almost an echo of Herodotus' description of Persian education as consisting of *τρία μοῦνα, ἱππεύειν καὶ τοξεύειν καὶ ἀληθίζεσθαι* (1.136), although it omits the third ingredient. He describes the Trojans (fr. 775 inc.; see above, p. 77) as,

> φίλιπποι καὶ κερουλκοί,
> σὺν σάκει δὲ κωδωνοκρότῳ παλαισταί.

The suggestion of contempt in the second line however is not at all like Herodotus.[24] It is scarcely necessary to refer fragment 823 (inc.) to Herodotus—

> ὠνὴν ἔθου καὶ πρᾶσιν ὡς Φοῖνιξ ἀνὴρ
> Σιδώνιος κάπηλος—

---

version (fr. 126 P = fr. 122 N *Andromeda*) is elaborately rearranged. But both Nauck and Pearson retain the key words, though in a different order. I give Nauck's as nearer the original.

> νόμος γάρ ἐστι τοῖς βαρβάροις θυηπολεῖν
> βροτεῖον . . . γέρος (γέρας?) τῷ Κρόνῳ.

According to Pearson's note ad loc., the Greeks identified Cronus with Moloch. Could Sophocles have an actual foreign god in mind, or is he merely thinking of the well-known child-eating propensities of Cronus in Greek myth? For the Phoenician origin of the family of Andromeda, see below p. 90.

23. This fragment is cited by O. Jessen (PW, *8*, 70, s.v. *Helios*) as the only authority for this practice. For a similar use of a fragment of Aeschylus, see above p. 43 with n. 32.

24. Vater, cited in *TGF*, p. 313, reflects the usual attitude toward Sophocles in his suggestion that Plutarch, to whom we owe the fragment, through a slip of the memory attributed

even if the historian does begin his book with a story about Phoenician merchants.[25]

A few fragments are much vaguer. Fragment 470 (*Poimenes*) speaks of the Βερέκυντα βρόμον of the Phrygian flute. We know from the context of fragment 778 (inc.) that Sophocles associated the Corybantes with the worship of Dionysus. But neither of these fragments tells us whether he presented the cults of the Phrygian mother or Dionysus in any detail. A fragment of *Laocoon* (341) gives a picture of the general richness of foreign ritual.

> λάμπει δ' ἀγυιεὺς βωμὸς ἀτμίζων πυρὶ
> σμύρνης σταλαγμούς, βαρβάρους εὐοσμίας.

It would be difficult to determine whether the Colchian spells of Medea (fr. 491–3 *Rhizotomoi*) could be distinguished from spells practiced in other countries.

The treatment of the history of the Pelasgians in *Inachus* (fr. 248) shows that Sophocles shares with Aeschylus an awareness of the artistic value of historical material, though we have no example in

---

lines to Sophocles that really belong to Euripides. The basis for this, aside from the conviction that Sophocles avoided references to foreigners, seems to be Euripides fr. 935 inc.,

ἀλλ' ὦ φίλιπποι Τρῶες.

25. This may well be a digression in a context where no foreigners are involved, like the reference to Egyptian custom in *OC*. All that is called for is a situation in which something that ought not to be sold has been put up for sale, e.g., the Greek brides of Procne's speech, who are "sold" (διεμπολώμεθα) by their fathers (fr. 524 *Tereus*).

Sophocles of this method applied to foreign history.

Two fragments from *Tereus* raise the question of the inferiority of foreigners. One (fr. 524) discusses the fate of a woman who marries a foreigner, and the other (fr. 528) speaks of the greed of barbarians, presumably Thracians. Thracian greed is attested by Thucydides (2.97).[26]

Some of the lost plays give us hints of how, in a more general way, foreign behavior was used thematically, or as a source of conflict or contrast. In this field inferences are extremely tenuous, but perhaps worth making because they can be so suggestive. For example, Pearson,[27] accepting Dindorf's suggestion that fragment 663 (N inc. = fr. 178 P) comes from *Helenes Apaitesis*, attributes to Helen the lines,

> *ἐμοὶ δὲ λῷστον αἷμα ταύρειον πιεῖν*
> *καὶ μὴ 'πὶ πλεῖον τῶνδ' ἔχειν δυσφημίας.*

(I give Pearson's text, instead of Nauck's, since I am presenting his theory.) If this is right, Sophocles could be referring to the death of Psamtik III (Hdt. 3.15) or, more suggestively, he may be comparing Helen's situation in Troy to that of Themistocles in Persia. In this theme of the Greek traitor living among foreigners the possibilities for developing and contrasting Greek and Persian-Trojan characters are very great.

Poimenes is another play which raises such specu-

26. The parallel is observed in Pearson's note to fr. 587 (= fr. 528 N *Tereus*).

27. See Pearson's note to fr. 178 (= fr. 663 N inc.).

lations. Its rustic messenger (fr. 461, probably also 462 and 463), its chorus of shepherds, from whom a good many of the outlandish expressions must certainly come—for example, ἰὼ βαλλήν (fr. 472), ψό (fr. 478), perhaps Γραῖκες (fr. 475), or Ἴαννα (fr. 476)—its coarse-spoken Cycnus (fr. 460), offer opportunities for elaborating not only on the foreignness, but also on the wildness and simplicity of such characters. Perhaps there was here something like the romantic simplicity of the natives in *Iphigenia Among the Taurians*, but with this important difference: the Euripidean primitives are essentially Greek rustics (see below, pp. 149–50), while it is clear that Sophocles' shepherds, whatever else they are, are foreigners in speech and behavior.[28]

In *Thamyras* too there are suggestions of a foreign theme. How, for instance, did Sophocles develop the twice expressed contrast between Greek and oriental musical instruments (fr. 217, 220)? Was this an important element in the theme of the conflict of Thamyras and the muses, or was it used to show Thamyras' difference from his Thracian subjects? Is fragment 219 perhaps a wild Thracian dance,[29] and is the reference to hemp (fr. 222) necessarily to hempen

28. Welcker (*Die griechischen Tragödien* [3 vols. Bonn, 1839–41], *1*, 116) compares *Poimenes* to *Rhesus* and *Persae*. Wilamowitz ("Lesefrüchte," *Hermes*, *61* [1926], 284) calls *Poimenes* the model for *Rhesus!* Both authors apparently observed the exotic atmosphere, but neither drew any general conclusions from it.

29. See Pearson note to fr. 240 (= fr. 219 N *Thamyras*).

cloth, or could it be the plant's intoxicating properties?[30] Certainly there is enough to suggest that Sophocles made something of a contrast between a wild and primitive Thracian(?) music and a more restrained Greek style.

In *Tereus* there is little doubt that foreignness is an important theme. As Pearson sees it, "it is important to remember that the gruesome history was enacted among a rude and savage people; and the terrible revenge exacted by the Athenian women shows the effect upon their character of alien surroundings and barbarous treatment."[31] This implies a careful characterization of Tereus as a Thracian, and a contrast of Thracian and Greek types. Of the fourteen fragments (fr. 523–38) five have some direct reference to this point. On the one hand we have the hostile tone of Procne's lament over the fate of women—married, without being consulted, into the homes of *ξένοι* and *βάρβαροι* (fr. 524);[32] her homesick cry (fr. 525),

> πολλά σε ζηλῶ βίου,
> μάλιστα δ' εἰ γῆς μὴ πεπείρασαι ξένης,

30. See Pearson note to fr. 243 (= fr. 222 N *Thamyras*).

31. Pearson, *2*, 225.

32. The authenticity of this speech has been questioned because of the Euripidean tone and a certain awkwardness of language (see Pearson's note to fr. 583 = fr. 524 N *Tereus*). But, as Pearson points out, these are not decisive arguments. The tone is certainly no more Euripidean than the nurse's speech in *Trachiniae* (899–946), or the character of Athena in *Ajax*.

and someone's angry comment (fr. 528),

> *φιλάργυρον μὲν πᾶν τὸ βάρβαρον γένος.*

On the other hand, without any such note of hostility is (fr. 523),

> *Ἥλιε, φιλίπποις Θρῃξὶ πρέσβιστον σέλας.*

One other passage bearing on this problem is neglected by Pearson (fr. 532).

> *ἓν φῦλον ἀνθρώπων μι' ἔδειξε πατρὸς* στρ.
> *καὶ ματρὸς ἡμᾶς ἁμέρα τοὺς πάντας· οὐδεὶς*
> *ἔξοχος ἄλλος ἔβλαστεν ἄλλου.*
> *βόσκει δὲ τοὺς μὲν μοῖρα δυσαμερίας,* ἀντ.
> *τοὺς δ' ὄλβος ἡμῶν, τοὺς δὲ δουλείας* ⏑ – –
> – ⏑ ⏑ – *ζυγὸν ἔσχ' ἀνάγκας.*

(The attempt to recover the strophic structure is Nauck's.) This puts the Greek barbarian conflict in a different light from the one in which Pearson sees it. The chorus, whether Greek or Thracian, affirms something quite different from what Procne has been saying—not the superiority of the Greeks, but the common humanity of all men. This seems to me to preclude a black and white opposition, such as Pearson suggests, between Greek and barbarian. Someone, possibly the chorus, points out that Procne and Philomela outdo Tereus in savagery (fr. 530).

> *ἄνους ἐκεῖνος· αἱ δ' ἀνουστέρως ἔτι*
> *ἐκεῖνον ἠμύναντο καρτερόν.*

> *ὅστις γὰρ ἐν κακοῖσι θυμωθεὶς βροτῶν*
> *μεῖζον προσάπτει τῆς νόσου τὸ φάρμακον,*
> *ἰατρός ἐστιν οὐκ ἐπιστήμων ἀκῶν.*

On Pearson's theory this is a degeneration of character brought about by Tereus' savage treatment of the sisters. But in view of the theme of universal humanity expressed by the chorus we should imagine the Greek-barbarian opposition as somewhat more complex. Perhaps Procne's violent repudiation of her new home was the original cause of Tereus' violence against Philomela. The chorus voices so many typically Greek sentiments (fr. 531, 533–4, 535–6) that it is difficult to imagine, with Jebb and Welcker, that they were Thracian women.[33] The argument is circular however, and those who disagree with my main thesis can reverse it and say that the fact that Thracian women talk like Greeks is evidence that Sophocles did not differentiate Greeks and foreigners. My own guess however is that Procne, like Iphigenia and Helen, had Greek attendants in her exile. But, whatever the details of treatment, clearly in this play the theme of foreignness was important.

In *Andromeda* too there is reason to detect, in addition to a good deal of foreign local color, a certain emphasis on the contrast between Greek and oriental in the characters of Perseus, the Greek deliverer, and Phineus or Agenor, the oriental betrothed, who, hav-

33. See Pearson's notes to fr. 589 and 591 *Tereus* = fr. 530 and 532 N.

ing deserted Andromeda at the moment of danger, returns to claim her hand after Perseus has rescued her. It is fairly certain that Sophocles built his play around the contest of Perseus and the other suitor for the hand of Andromeda.[34] This situation invites the contrast of Greek and barbarian.

Our evidence that Sophocles did in fact develop this contrast rests mainly on a theory of Petersen's that a hydria in the British Museum represents Sophocles' version of the story.[35] On the vase three national types are represented—Greek, oriental, Ethiopian. The Greek is Perseus in traditional winged cap, chlamys, and sandals. There are two orientals, wearing what seem to be variants of Persian royal dress (see above, p. 28 with n. 13). One is seated, and wears tiara, long sleeveless chiton, himation, and shoes that seem to be tied with bows. The other is leaning on two slaves, and wears tiara, short sleeveless chiton, and under it a sort of spotted leotard reaching to wrists and ankles. He has shoes like the other Persian. There are eight Ethiopian slaves with curly black hair and negroid features, all wearing short, highly decorated sleeveless chitons. As Petersen interprets the picture, the seated figure is Cepheus mourning his daughter's approaching fate, the standing oriental is Phineus, leaning on two slaves because he is too languid and effeminate to walk

34. Pearson, *1*, 79, and E. Petersen, "Andromeda," *J.H.S.*, *24* (1904), 110–12.

35. Petersen, ibid., 105–8. Cf. Schmid-Stählin, I², 435 with n. 13, and O. Wernicke in PW, *1*, 2154 ff, s.v. *Andromeda.*

by himself, the other slaves are engaged in preparations for the sacrifice of Andromeda. The vase painter has heavily underlined the foreign theme. If Petersen is right, we may guess that Sophocles did too, making the most of the scenic and dramatic possibilities in a story involving native Ethiopians, an oriental royal family, and a Greek knight errant.

We may ask how Phineus and Cepheus come to be represented as Persians. There are three traditions about the location of the story of Andromeda. Cepheus and Phineus are sons of the Phoenician Belus, and according to some versions the events of Andromeda's exposure and rescue take place at Joppa in their native land. The more usual version—that of Euripides for example—is that Cepheus has become king of the Ethiopians, and the story takes place there. But according to Herodotus (7.61, 150) Cepheus was king of the Cephenes in Persia, and brought up Perses, son of Perseus and Andromeda. The Cephenes changed their name to Persians when Cepheus made Perses his heir.[36] Since we would expect Sophocles to use Herodotus' version of the story, this tends to substantiate Petersen's theory. It is interesting that one of the few fragments of the play contains the word *σάρητον*, a name for the Persian tunic with the white panel which was part of the royal apparel (see above, pp. 69–70). In the vase painting the chiton of Phineus has a panel,

36. See Latte in PW, *11*, 222, s.v. *Kephenes* and *Kepheus;* also Aeschylus *Pers.* 79 and schol. ad loc. In Herodotus (6.54) the Persians call Perses an Assyrian.

not white however, but spotted, the vase painter's imaginative version of a σάρητον?

These are suggestions rather than proofs, but they do tempt me to suppose that Sophocles is here again following Herodotus, and really did represent Andromeda and her family as Persian royalty. As to the Ethiopian slaves of the hydria, I can only wonder whether Sophocles imported them into Persia, or conflated two traditions and exported his Persians to Ethiopia. Could he have made the royal family Phoenicians or Ethiopians who wore the σάρητον as a sort of conventional dress for all orientals? This last seems very unlikely in view of the care Sophocles took to represent foreigners accurately. Since Herodotus (3.22) tells us that the king of Ethiopia expressed the greatest contempt for the Persian garment (πορφύρειον εἶμα) which Cambyses sent him, it is unlikely that Sophocles would have been so careless as to dress Ethiopians in the typically Persian σάρητον.[37] To those who accept my thesis about Sophocles, this argument, fanciful and undemonstrable as it is, will have a certain cogency. To those who prefer the traditional view

37. It is tempting to imagine that Sophocles also followed Herodotus (2.29–30; 3.17–26, 997, 114; 7.69) in contrasting the powerful plain-living Ethiopians with the luxurious Persians. The vase painter, it is true, makes them smaller than the Persians, while Herodotus (3.20) calls them μέγιστοι καὶ κάλλιστοι ἀνθρώπων πάντων. However the painter *does* make a strong contrast between the energy of the Ethiopians, and the languor of Phineus whom they support. But this is pure speculation.

that Sophocles was basically not interested in foreigners, it will seem more plausible that he should have committed the boner of dressing a Phoenician or Ethiopian in a Persian tunic.

This discussion could probably be extended to include all the lost plays that deal with foreigners. For instance what are we to think of the mourning scene in *Eurypylus* (fr. 210, 211 P),[38] or the romantic enchantress Medea revealed to us by the fragments of *Colchides* (fr. 312, 315, 316), and *Rhizotomoi* (fr. 491–3)? [39] But perhaps enough examples have been

38. For fragments of Eurypylus it is necessary to refer to Pearson, since the publication of the papyrus containing them and *Ichneutae* is later than *TGF*.

39. Fr. 491 (*Rhizotomoi*) is cited by Macrobius (*Saturnalia*, 5.19, 9, quoted in *TGF*, p. 249) as the source of some of the magic paraphernalia in *Aeneid* 4.513 ff. Certainly the romantic feeling is closer to that of Vergil, and the similar passages in Apollonius (see schol. *Argonautica* 3.1372; 4.223; and Welcker, *Die griechische Tragödien*, *1*, 335) and Ovid (*Metamorphoses* 7.179–349) than to what is usually called the Sophoclean spirit. In this connection it is seldom observed how little the fantastic story of Nessus, and the details of the magic practiced on the shirt, in *Trachiniae* consort with this assumed spirit. Were such an episode introduced into either Oedipus play, what a violation of the emphasis on "man for his own sake" it would be. This raises a point not strictly relevant to my discussion, namely, the extent to which romance and marvels, not necessarily involving foreign material, were employed in the lost plays. There was not apparently very much fabulous geography (see below, p. 100), but there were a good many magical effects, e.g., Triptolemus' dragon chariot (fr. 539 *Triptolemus*), the metamorphosis of Tereus and Procne (Aristophanes, *Birds* 99–100 and schol. ad loc.,

given to suggest the possibility that Sophocles not only attempted realism in the portrayal of foreigners, but also, in a more general way, built their characteristics and personalities into the structure of his plays.

It is the fragments again, rather than the extant plays, that give us our information. From them it is clear that in representing barbarians Sophocles was not content with a few vaguely exotic touches, but was at pains to acquire quite specific and definite information about the different peoples he dealt with. On the basis of fragments alone we cannot tell how extensively and consistently he developed the exotic element. But, judging from the number and quality of the surviving references, we may conclude that, though he may have done less of this than Aeschylus, he certainly did more than we would have guessed from the evidence of the extant plays. The question of the inferiority of foreigners does not seem to be a major preoccupation with Sophocles, but it was raised and discussed in at least two plays, *Ajax* and *Tereus*.

---

quoted in *TGF*, p. 257), the ghost of Achilles in *Polyxena* (fr. 480), the brazen bulls of Colchis (fr. 312 *Colchides*). This material raises the same question as the material about foreigners: does it belong to an early Aeschylean period, or does it appear in plays of more than one period (see below, pp. 104–11)? The answer of course depends on our ability to date the fragments in which the references occur. In view of the fact that *Philoctetes* (409 B.C.) ends with a *deus ex machina*, I am inclined to think, until the contrary is proved, that magical episodes are not limited to the early period.

Geography

In the extant plays, Sophocles on the whole avoids specific reference to geographical facts, either foreign or Greek. Even the Colonus ode (*OC* 668–719) is more of a spiritual tribute than a description. There are however a few vague references to foreign places. Purely conventional references are rare. In this category we might place Thracian storms (*OT* 197; *Ant.* 589), the rough Cretan sea (*Trach.* 118–19), golden Pactolus (*Phil.* 394), Sardian electrum and Indian gold (*Ant.* 1037–8), Phasis and Ister as types of great rivers (*OT* 1227). All these are introduced, not because the story requires a reference to a particular place, but as types of the exotic, of rough weather, of wealth, and so forth. They convey no special information, and may be regarded as formulaic.

A few other passages, though not purely stock, lack Aeschylus' vividness and concreteness. For example (*Ant.* 966–70),

> παρὰ δὲ κυανέαιν σπιλάδοιν διδύμας ἁλὸς
> ἀκταὶ Βοσπόριαι ἰδ' ὁ Θρῃκῶν <ἠιὼν>
> Σαλμυδησσός, ἵν' ἀγχίπολις Ἄρης . . .

The outlandish names give an effect of distance and loneliness, but the scene itself is not definite or easily visualized. Again, in *Trachiniae*, Sophocles ignores the opportunity offered by the myth of Heracles to turn geography into poetry and drama. One of the few geographical references in the play comes when the chorus hopes that the sun, looking down on the world, may know where Heracles is (*Trach.* 99–101).

> ὦ λαμπρᾷ στεροπᾷ φλεγέθων,
> ἢ ποντίας αὐλῶνας, ἢ
> δισσαῖσιν ἀπείροις κλιθείς.

The passage shows the general Greek view of the two mainlands, but gives us none of Aeschylus' concrete information about their boundaries and relation to each other. The same generalized approach appears in the reference to the four quarters of the earth (*OC* 1244–8),

> ἆται κλονέουσιν ἀεὶ συνοῦσαι,
> αἱ μὲν ἀπ' ἀελίου δυσμᾶν,
> αἱ δ' ἀνατέλλοντος,
> αἱ δ' ἀνὰ μέσσαν ἀκτῖν',
> αἱ δ' ἐννυχιᾶν ἀπὸ Ῥιπᾶν.

The streams of Bosporus (*Ajax* 884; see above, p. 56), the damp climate of the Troad (*Ajax* 1206–10), Aetnaean ponies (*OC* 312) are mere passing references.

This is a thin collection in comparison with Aeschylus' *Suppliants*, *Persae*, and *Prometheus*. But if we except these three "foreign" plays and compare Sophocles' plays with *Seven* and *Oresteia*, it turns out that Sophocles falls into foreign geographical digressions slightly more often than Aeschylus (see Appendix).

The fragments, on the other hand, are much richer in foreign geography. Sophocles names 61 foreign peoples and places, as compared with Aeschylus' 100. About a fifth of the names in Aeschylus occur only in the fragments. More than half of the names in Sophocles occur only in the fragments (see Appendix). Since we have to rely so much on fragments it is harder to get a picture of Sophocles' geography, but the evidence indicates that it was a good deal more extensive than the extant plays would lead us to suppose.

In *Triptolemus* Sophocles appears to have used the journey motif much as Aeschylus did in *Prometheus*. Strabo (1.27) criticizes the account of Triptolemus' journey, together with the prologue of *Bacchae*, for disregarding geographical order. In describing the journey of Dionysus and his followers Euripides is not interested in the route, but in the exotic effect of the names of distant and little known places. Nevertheless the journey is not as impossible to visualize as Strabo implies (see below, p. 164). In the case of *Triptolemus* the criticism is even less justified. A surviving fragment of *Triptolemus*, and a comment of Dionysius of Halicarnassus, do not support Strabo's criticism of Sophocles' geography in this play.[40] Demeter tells Triptolemus what his route through the world will be (fr. 541 *Triptolemus*),

> τὰ δ' ἐξόπισθε χειρὸς εἰς τὰ δεξιὰ
> Οἰνωτρία τε πᾶσα καὶ Τυρσηνικὸς
> κόλπος Λιγυστική τε γῆ σε δέξεται.

40. Kranz (*Stasimon*, pp. 108–9) also rejects Strabo's criticism, though on other grounds than mine, namely, that Strabo cannot praise any poet except Homer.

This is a fairly systematic and well visualized description of the shores of the Tyrrhenian sea. Dionysius (*Antiquitates Romanae*, 1.12, quoted in *TGF*, p. 262) bears out this view. He says that Sophocles describes the east of Italy from Iapygia to the Sicilian strait, then Sicily, and then returns to western Italy and *goes through* (διεξέρχεται) the more important tribes of the coast, deriving them from the settlement of Oenotrians. This certainly suggests a clear picture of the geography and peoples of Italy and Sicily.[41] It implies an itinerary not like the Bacchants', but like Io's, presented in geographical order with comments on the places and peoples on the road. And in fact Sophocles seems to echo Prometheus' words to Io (*PV* 789; Sophocles fr. 540 *Triptolemus*), as though to suggest that he is going to present a journey speech in the Aeschylean manner. Other fragments of *Triptolemus*, discussed below, give information about Triptolemus' route which is comparable to the information about Io's route—rice cake (fr. 552), silphium (fr. 546), beer (fr. 553), the grain fields of Italy (fr. 543).[42]

41. Pearson's note to fr. 598 (= 541 N *Triptolemus*), though it does not expressly deal with the question, implies that the geography of the passage is on the whole accurate and intelligible.

42. Comparison of the journeys of Io and Triptolemus is a commonplace of criticism. See Pohlenz, *Griechische Tragödie*, *1*, 170; Kranz, *Stasimon*, p. 81; Pearson, *2*, 239 and note to fr. 597 = fr. 537 N *Triptolemus;* W. Schmid, *Untersuchungen zum gefesselten Prometheus*, p. 58. The fairly general assumption that Sophocles is here challenging Aeschylus on his own ground suggests that Strabo's criticism is unfounded. The

We find various bits of curious geographical information in the fragments. Sophocles, like Aeschylus, attributed the flooding of the Nile to melting snows (fr. 797 inc.; see above, p. 55). Apparently he also agreed with Aeschylus about the boundaries of Europe and Asia. The scholiast says (see above, pp. 50–3 with n. 44) that both writers regarded Tanais as the boundary. Since we know from Aeschylus' own words that he makes this boundary Phasis, we can guess that the scholiast has mistaken his rivers, and should have said Phasis.

Sophocles locates the Idaean Dactyls in Phrygia (fr. 337 *Kophoi Satyroi*). He makes the original Pelasgians Tyrrhenians (fr. 248 *Inachus*), and we have seen (above, p. 97) that he derives the Italians from Oenotrians.

Of foreign creatures we hear of two mentioned also by Aeschylus—the Aetnaean beetle (fr. 165 *Daedalus;* fr. 314 P *Ichneutae,* 300), and the βούβαλις, or African antelope (fr. 724 inc.; see above, p. 59). Then there are the mules of Acesta (fr. 611 *Hydrophoroi*), and possibly the Indian ants (fr. 26 *Aethiopes*) described by Herodotus (3.102).[43]

---

echo of *PV* cannot, of course, be certainly linked to the journey speech, but its presence at the least suggests that Sophocles had Io's journey in mind when he was writing the play; unless we should assume that Aeschylus is imitating Sophocles!

43. This more than doubtful fragment is so interpreted by Nauck (*TGF,* ad loc.), and Pearson in his note to fr. 29

Of natural products the fragments mention a meadow of silphium (fr. 546 *Triptolemus*), the rice cake (fr. 552 *Triptolemus*); λίβανος (fr. 961 inc.), Arabian incense; βάκκαρις (fr. 929 inc.), incense; a νεκυομαντεῖον in Etruria (fr. 682 inc.); and the Lydian stone, or magnet (fr. 732 inc.). All these are specific things that belong to some definite locality.

A few slightly longer passages remind us that Sophocles too could create detailed and vivid foreign scenes. Two fragments of *Poimenes* (fr. 462 and 463) describe fishing in the Bosporus region (see above, p. 56).

> ἔνθ' ἡ πάροικος πηλαμὺς χειμάζεται
> πάραυλος Ἑλλησποντίς, ὡραία θέρους
> τῷ Βοσπορίτῃ· τῷδε γὰρ θαμίζεται,

and

> κημοῖσι πλεκτοῖς πορφύρας φθείρει γένος.

He pictures a strange race of men who harvest strange fishes in a dangerous sea. The atmosphere is not specifically foreign however—more like the wild landscapes of *Iphigenia Among the Taurians* than like Aeschylus' precise scenes. Pliny (*Naturalis Historia*, 18.65, quoted in *TGF*, p. 263) translates for us a picture of the grain fields of Italy (fr. 543 *Triptolemus*).

> . . . Sophocles poeta in fabula Triptolemo frumentum Italicum ante cuncta laudaverit, ad ver-

(= fr. 26 N *Aethiopes*), and Rasch (*Sophocles quid debeat Herodoto*, p. 103).

> bum translata sententia "et fortunatam Italiam frumento canere candido."

This has something of the brilliance and concreteness of Aeschylus' description of the eruption of Aetna (see above, pp. 57–8).

In Sophocles there seems to be less of that fabulous geography which Aeschylus delights in. There is a brief reference to the sirens (fr. 777 inc.), to the brazen bulls of Colchis (fr. 312 *Colchides*), to the legendary lands beyond the sea where are the springs of night and heaven and the gardens of Phoebus (fr. 870 inc.), to the dragon of the Hesperides (*Trach.* 1100), to the cave of Atlas (fr. 314 P *Ichneutae*, 261), to the Rhipaean mountains (*OC* 1248). And there are the titles of two lost plays, *Phaeacians* and *Nausicaa*, which must at least have mentioned the lands of fable.

The fragments of Sophocles do not equal those of Aeschylus in quantity and detail of geographical information, but they still show a wide range of precise and curious knowledge about foreign peoples and places. In at least one case—the journey speech of *Triptolemus*—Sophocles shows the kind of geographical imagination we associate particularly with Aeschylus. There are fewer purely conventional geographical phrases than there are in Aeschylus, and less fabulous geography. In representing foreign places Sophocles is sometimes vague, but often he uses concrete details that apply to specific foreign places. In geography, as in other matters relating to foreign peoples, the fragments show that he has made much greater use of foreign local color than one would guess from the extant plays.[44]

Troy and Persia

I have already suggested (above, pp. 71–2) that Sophocles' Trojans and Phrygians sometimes turn out to be Persians.[45] Now that the different aspects of his representation of foreign peoples and places have been discussed, the question of the special place of Trojans in the plays of Sophocles can be considered in more detail. Tecmessa, Sophocles' only extant Trojan character, is not particularly exotic. She has more in common with the Greek-mannered Trojans of Euripides

44. Sophocles' interest in geography is briefly noted by Wilamowitz in a passage already referred to (above, n. 9), *Einleitung in die attische Tragödie*, p. 31 with n. 57 and p. 32.

45. Phrygian and Trojan are used as synonyms in Greek tragedy, a fact observed by Strabo (12.573), who asserts that the confusion about the boundaries in the region of the Troad is partly *διὰ τὰς τῶν συγγραφέων ἀνομολογίας, περὶ τῶν αὐτῶν οὐ τὰ αὐτὰ λεγόντων, τοὺς μὲν Τρῶας καλούντων Φρύγας, καθάπερ οἱ τραγικοί*. . . . (Cf. also 10.473; 14.675). Illustrations of this practice can be found in quantity in *Cyc.*, *Andr.*, *Hec.*, *Tro.*, *El.*, *Helen*, *Or.* of Euripides. One of his most frequent synonyms for Troy is *Φρυγῶν πόλις, γαῖα, χθών* (see below, p. 156). Troy and Phrygia are synonyms in Aeschylus only in fr. 446 inc.; in Sophocles only in *Ajax* 1054; fr. 339 *Lacaenae;* fr. 344 *Laocoon.* The small number of extant examples in Aeschylus and Sophocles can be attributed to the smaller number of extant plays involving Trojans, and to the fact that formulaic repetition of foreign names is not an important dramatic device with them as it is with Euripides.

than with Aeschylus' foreign princess, Cassandra. She is helpless and friendless not because she is a foreigner, but because she is a prisoner of war. But, as usual, the fragments give us quite another picture of Sophocles' handling of Trojan setting and characters. Here we see a more barbaric Troy—not just the conventionally rich and luxurious Troy of Euripides, but a Troy where (fr. 341 *Laocoon*)

> λάμπει δ' ἀγυιεὺς βωμὸς ἀτμίζων πυρὶ
> σμύρνης σταλαγμούς, βαρβάρους εὐοσμίας.

The Idaean Dactyls are Phrygians, devisers of the working of iron and other skills (fr. 337 *Kophoi Satyroi*); the Trojan royalty employ eunuchs (fr. 563 *Troilus*); Trojans carry shields hung with bells (fr. 775 inc.); and, most significant, Trojans speak a foreign language which in general character is the language of Aeschylus' Persians. They use Ἴαννα of a Greek woman (fr. 53 *Aechmalotides;* fr. 476 *Poimenes*), and Γραῖκες of Greek women (fr. 475 *Poimenes*); they refer to παρασάγγης (fr. 477 *Poimenes*), ὀροσάγγαι (fr. 184 *Helenes Gamos;* fr. 577 *Troilus*), βαλλήν (fr. 472 *Poimenes*), βαρίβας (fr. 474 *Poimenes*), σκαλμή (fr. 563 *Troilus*). They use the exclamation ψό (fr. 478 *Poimenes*), and the lament ἰαί (fr. 574 *Troilus*). Mysians also have Persian characteristics, if we may judge from τιάρα and σισυρνώδης στολή (fr. 379 *Mysi;* the meanings and provenience of these words are discussed above, pp. 68–72). Sophocles' Trojans speak a Persian language, refer to Persian objects, and observe Persian customs, or what passed for Persian among 5th century Greeks instructed by Aeschylus, Hecataeus, and Herodotus. If this had not been a fairly general practice with Sophocles, so many examples could not have survived in the fragments.

Sophocles apparently had a preference for Trojan subjects.[46] In addition to *Philoctetes*, *Electra*, and *Ajax*, he wrote 30 plays involving the Trojan story to some extent. Euripides wrote about 14, Aeschylus 14 (this includes the *Oresteia* trilogy) as well as we can judge from the surviving titles.[47] In another section we have

46. It is customary, at least since Athenaeus (7.277e; cf. also *Vita Sophoclis*, 12), to take note of Sophocles' preference for stories from the cyclic epics. See Pearson, *Fragments of Sophocles*, *1*, xxiii, and "The *Rhesus*," *Classical Review*, *35* (1921), 60; Schmid-Stählin, I², 326 and 437; Blumenthal in PW, *3* A, 1050, s.v. *Sophocles*. A great many of these stories, e.g., the whole Theban cycle, have no connection with Troy. So far as I can find out, his particular interest in Troy has gone unobserved. H. Degen (*De Troianis scaenicis*) has studied the general problem of Trojans in Greek drama, and observed that Sophocles and Euripides tend to assimilate Trojans to Persians. But Sophocles' far greater interest and more detailed and realistic presentation seem to have escaped him. The fact that Sophocles represents Trojan and Phrygian as Persian is noticed also by Welcker (*Die griechischen Tragödien*, *1*, 113), and Rasch (*Sophocles quid debeat Herodoto*, p. 114); but again without observing their special prominence in the plays of Sophocles.

47. In addition to *Ajax*, *Electra*, and *Philoctetes* the following 30 lost plays are connected more or less directly with some aspect of the Trojan story—*Achaion Syllogos*, *Aechmalotides*, *Aethiopes*, *Aias Lokros*, *Alexander*, *Andromache*, *Antenoridae*, *Chryses*, *Eurypylus*, *Helenes Apaitesis*, *Helenes Gamos*,

seen that none of the three dramatists had a special preference for myths dealing with barbarians (see above, pp. 7–9). But Sophocles, it appears, leaned more toward Trojan barbarians than did Aeschylus and Euripides. And we know that, at least in some cases, he represented them realistically, if unhistorically and anachronistically, as Persians. This is realism at the expense of truth—an unHerodotean aspect of this in some ways Herodotean writer. This evidence of a consistently visualized Phrygian world, modelled more or less on the Persia of Aeschylus and Herodotus, is in strong contrast to the view of Sophocles' handling of Trojans that we get from the extant plays.

Chronology

Before going on to conclude that the large amount of foreign material in the fragments of Sophocles must

---

Helenes Harpage, *Iphigeneia*, *Lacaenae*, *Laocoon*, *Memnon*, *Nauplius Katapleon*, *Nauplius Pyrkaeus*, *Odysseus Mainomenos*, *Palamedes*, *Philoctetes in Troy*, *Phryges*, *Poimenes*, *Polyxena*, *Priam*, *Scyrii*, *Sinon*, *Syndeipnon Achaion*, *Teucer*, *Troilus*—a total of 33 plays. Some of them, of course, may have had no Trojan characters, like *Philoctetes*, or Trojan characters like Tecmessa, whose foreign qualities have been soft-pedalled. There are only 14 plays of Aeschylus with stories related to the Trojan story, the 3 plays of Oresteia and 11 lost plays—*Hoplon Krisis*, *Iphigeneia*, *Memnon*, *Myrmidones*, *Nereides*, *Palamedes*, *Philoctetes*, *Phryges*, *Proteus*, *Psychostasia*, *Threissae*. Euripides had 14 plays on this subject, 6 lost plays—*Alexander*, *Epeius*, *Palamedes*, *Philoctetes*, *Protesilaus*, *Scyrii;* and 8 extant plays—*Andromache*, *Hecuba*, *Troiades*, *IA*, *IT*, *Helen*, *Electra*, *Orestes*.

alter rather drastically the traditional views about his style, we should consider for a moment the way in which the existence of this material is usually disposed of—namely, the theory of an early "Aeschylean" period in which the young Sophocles, under the powerful influence of the old master, imitated Aeschylus' colorful foreign effects. A much quoted passage in Plutarch (*Moralia, quo. quis sent. prof. virt.* 7) tells us that Sophocles himself believed he had at first imitated Aeschylus, and only gradually evolved his own style.

> *ὥσπερ γὰρ ὁ Σοφοκλῆς ἔλεγε τὸν Αἰσχύλου διαπεπαιχὼς ὄγκον' εἶτα τὸ πικρὸν καὶ κατάτεχνον τῆς αὐτοῦ κατασκευῆς' τρίτον ἤδη τὸ τῆς λέξεως μεταβάλλειν εἶδος, ὅπερ ἠθικώτατόν ἐστι καὶ βέλτιστον, οὕτως οἱ φιλοσοφοῦντες, ὅταν ἐκ τῶν πανηγυρικῶν καὶ κατατέχνων εἰς τὸν ἁπτόμενον ἤθους καὶ πάθους λόγον μεταβῶσιν, ἄρχονται τὴν ἀληθῆ προκοπὴν προκόπτειν καὶ ἄτυφον.*

Such scraps of foreign lore as investigators bother to cite are usually written off as juvenilia belonging to this first period (see above, p. 72 with n. 9). One would assume then (1) that there is not very much foreign material in Sophocles, (2) that most of it can be assigned to early plays, (3) that the realistic portrayal of foreign peoples and places is a significant element in the Aeschylean *ὄγκος*. Point one is clearly wrong, and I believe I can show that there is no certainty about the other two.

As far as point one goes, the foreign material in Sophocles' fragments has never, so far as I know, been assembled in one place. Rasch's study is perhaps the fullest, but it ignores foreign material that is not Herodotean, and discusses Herodotean material that is not foreign. Therefore it has been easy for investigators to pass the foreign material off as negligible, with a general reference to *Triptolemus* and the passage on the Nile flood (fr. 797 inc.), as though this were the whole story. Anyone who looks at all the material together must acknowledge that, whatever period or periods of his life produced it, it is no small proportion of Sophocles' total work.

Point two brings us to the question of the dates of the lost plays—a subject too complex for me to do justice to here. However, the facts—as opposed to conjectures and theories—of the case are few and easily stated. It is almost certain that one of the plays Sophocles presented in 468 B.C.—his first competition—was *Triptolemus*.[48] This is the fact on which most of the theories about the nature of the early Aeschylean style are built. It is more than probable that *Thamyras*, another play very rich in foreign material, was also an early play, since Sophocles himself performed in it.[49] But what of the other plays from which we have cited foreign material? *Andromeda* is assumed to be earlier than 412 B.C., since it is thought to pre-

48. Schmid-Stählin, I^2, 313, and Blumenthal in PW, *3* A, 1076.

49. *Vita Sophoclis*, 4, Athenaeus, 1.20 ff.

cede Euripides' *Andromeda*.[50] It has been argued that *Oenomaus* is late because the fragments have a Euripidean tone.[51] *Tereus* is parodied in Aristophanes' *Birds* (100 and schol. ad loc.), and is therefore presumed to be earlier than 414 B.C. If it is to belong to the period of Sophocles' youth we must put it *at least* forty years earlier than the play that parodies it, but this is not unthinkable.[52] The Euripidean tone of Procne's lament is usually used as an argument for assigning it a late date.[53] There are no clues to the dates of the other foreign plays I have discussed. For four plays that *may* have contained foreign material we have some hints at dates. *Nausicaa*, like *Thamyras*, is probably early, since Sophocles appeared in it himself.[54] *Lemniae* is probably early, since it contained a catalogue of Argonauts imitated from *Cabiri* of Aeschylus.[55] *Chryses*, like *Tereus*, is referred to in *Birds* (1240), and must therefore be earlier than 414 B.C. One of the two Phineus

50. Schmid-Stählin, I², 436.
51. Ibid., p. 440.
52. *Wasps* 1087, for example,

εἶτα δ' εἰπόμεσθα θυννάζοντες εἰς τοὺς θυλάκους,

seems to be intended to remind the audience of Aeschylus' *Persae* 424,

τοὶ δ' ὥς τε θύννους ἤ τιν' ἰχθύων βόλον
ἀγαῖσι κωπῶν θραύμασιν τ' ἐρειπίων
ἔπαιον ἐρράχιζον·

although the two plays are more than fifty years apart.

53. Schmid-Stählin, I², 452.
54. Ibid., p. 442.
55. Ibid., p. 431.

plays was produced in the late twenties of the 5th century.[56] We have no way of knowing whether any of these four plays developed the foreign elements in the myths involved. In other words, the argument comes down to this, that *Triptolemus* and *Thamyras* are probably early and *Oenomaus* and *Tereus* are probably late. This seems to me not a very strong case for the theory that foreign local color is confined to the early plays that imitated Aeschylus.[57]

The third point, that ὄγκος and σεμνότης when applied to Aeschylus refer particularly to realistic representation of foreign peoples and places such as we find in *Suppliants*, *Persae*, and *Prometheus*, is also open to doubt. There is general agreement from Aristophanes on that ὄγκος and σεμνότης are characteristic of Aeschylus' style, but perhaps our ideas of the content of those terms have been distorted by the preponderance of foreign material in the plays that have survived into modern times. I have already pointed out that foreign material is confined to a rather small number of Aeschylus' plays, and that it is something of an accident that the plays we know happen to have so much (see above, p. 61). Presumably a reader who knew the whole body of his work would not immediately think of what Kranz calls his "orientalizing." From Aristotle we learn what τὸ μὴ ταπεινόν [σεμνότης] consists of

56. Ibid., p. 429.

57. Those who, like Cedric Whitman (*Sophocles*, pp. 44 ff), date *Ajax* in this early Aeschylean period will have to explain Tecmessa. She is not foreign enough.

(*Poetics*, 1458a, 18–1459a, 16). It depends on τὸ ξενικόν. ξενικὸν δὲ λέγω γλῶτταν καὶ μεταφορὰν καὶ ἐπέκτασιν καὶ πᾶν τὸ παρὰ τὸ κύριον (1458a, 21–23). Τὸ ξενικὸν is not "foreign" in the sense that we have been using the word, but unfamiliar. We know from the examples that follow that γλῶτται are not usually foreign words, but Greek words not in daily use; for example, θοινᾶται instead of ἐσθίει. From which we may conclude that the vocabulary of *Seven* may be just as lofty in Aristotle's sense as that of *Persae* or *Suppliants*. And in fact Aristophanes quotes this play as an example of loftiness (*Frogs* 1019–21). Aristophanes too gives us little reason to suppose that the bristling and turbid might which he attributes to the style of Aeschylus, in contrast to the finicky exactness of that of Euripides, is in any important way derived from the use of foreign material. It is true, Aeschylus is accused of partiality for monsters such as one finds ἐν τοῖς παραπετάσμασιν τοῖς Μηδικοῖς (*Frogs* 938). But here we are dealing with the fabulous rather than with known facts about foreign peoples. The monster Cycnus and the terrible warrior Memnon are cited, not because they are foreign, but because they terrify (*Frogs* 961–3). *Persae* is cited as an example of how to instill the desire for victory, though Dionysus adds a compliment on the style of the Persian lament for Darius (*Frogs* 1025–9). The ὄγκος of Aeschylus seems to depend on obscurity, solemnity, repetition, polysyllabic words, and the social importance of his ideas. As Aeschylus himself says (*Frogs* 1058–9), when accused of putting Lycabettus and hunks of Parnassus into his verse,

ἀνάγκη
μεγάλων γνωμῶν καὶ διανοιῶν ἴσα καὶ τὰ ῥήματα τίκτειν.

Indeed, it is Euripides not Aeschylus who is accused of foreign effects (*Frogs* 1301–7), and throughout the scene the running attack on Cleophon's Thracian ancestry, and the contrasting of it with the manly Greek sentiments of Aeschylus, make it seem very unlikely that Aristophanes regards the use of foreign material as characteristically Aeschylean.[58]

There is not much evidence, then, either in the plays of Aeschylus or in the comments of Aristotle and Aristophanes, for the assumption that ὄγκος implies the elaboration of foreign material either in style or content. I myself find it easier to believe that when Sophocles speaks of imitating the ὄγκος of Aeschylus in his youth, he is thinking rather of the massive dignity and rugged solemnity which Aristophanes parodies for us. The catalogue of *Lemniae*, or the journey

58. After writing this discussion of ὄγκος I discovered that C. M. Bowra interprets it in substantially the same way (*Problems in Greek Poetry*, Ch. 7, "Sophocles on His Own Development" [Oxford, 1953], pp. 112–17). Though he uses *Triptolemus* to illustrate Sophoclean ὄγκος, he does not give undue weight to the foreign material. I differ with Bowra however in his attempt to show that expression (λέξις) is emphasized by Sophocles only in his description of his third period. It seems to me that, while change in expression obviously reflects some change in interest and content, Sophocles, in describing his three phases, is at all times more concerned with expression than with content.

speech of *Triptolemus*, might well be included under this heading, but not so much because of foreign content as because of the weighty effect such lists are apt to have. The foreign material of the fragments seems to me too extensive and too complicated to explain by relegating it to an experimental youthful period. It seems far more likely that, from time to time throughout his life, Sophocles drew on his rather large and accurate store of knowledge, in order to include realistically foreign characters in plays where it suited his purpose to do so. Sophocles' own description of his later style implies that this was the case. A style which paid more attention to character would require that foreigners, wherever they appeared, should be suitably characterized.[59] If it is true that he owes a great deal of the information he uses in this process to his association with Herodotus, we should not expect to find most of it in the earliest plays, but rather in those that belong to the time of Herodotus' sojourn in Athens, or after it.[60]

Conclusion

But regardless of chronology, our estimate of Sophocles needs some modification. We have accustomed ourselves to think of Sophocles, in contrast to Euripi-

59. For this view of the meaning of ἠθικώτατον see Bowra, "Sophocles on His Own Development," pp. 121–3.

60. The implications of the relationship to Herodotus for the dating of the plays of Sophocles are discussed by Rasch (*Sophocles quid debeat Herodoto*, p. 123), and F. Jacoby (PW, Suppl. 2, p. 236, s.v. *Herodotos*).

des and Aeschylus, as "pure Greek." The extant plays limit themselves more or less closely to Greek problems and subjects, neglecting every opportunity for achieving effects from foreign local color. There are none of Aeschylus' barbaric sound effects, no gorgeous choruses like those of *Bacchae* and *Persae*, no untamed natures like Medea's. He never distracts from the problems of *man* by introducing foreign *men* in unfamiliar surroundings. But the fragments show us another Sophocles. Statistically, we have the fact that the fragments have three times as many foreign words as the fragments of Aeschylus; that they refer to more foreign customs and objects than those of Aeschylus; and of names of foreign people and places they contain ten more than the fragments of Aeschylus. As with Aeschylus, the distribution of these names between fragments and extant plays is significant. Aeschylus' fragments contain only about one-fifth of the names of people and places he uses. More than one-half of those used by Sophocles occur only in the fragments (see Appendix for statistics on names of foreign people and places). These are only a few of many indications that our picture of the two writers' handling of foreign material is a result of the accidents of survival. If Sophocles' *Poimenes*, *Triptolemus*, and *Andromeda* had survived, and Aeschylus' *Persae*, *Suppliants*, and *Prometheus* had not, our impression might have been reversed.[61]

61. The following passage from the anonymous hypothesis to *Rhesus* seems to me to indicate that ancient critics, who

Since we have only fragments to deal with, we cannot be too certain of the extent or the handling of this foreign material. However a few things are clear. Formulaic and decorative use of foreign words is rare in Sophocles. While he is less addicted to foreign geography than Aeschylus, he does at times show the same kind of topographical precision and detail, notably in *Triptolemus*. In his avoidance of fabulous lore about the remote parts of the world—if we can rely on our evidence—he differs from Aeschylus, and shows, perhaps, not only the tendency of his generation, but also his own particular bias toward the more scientific criteria of truth set up by Herodotus.

---

knew Sophocles by many more works than we do, did not think of Sophocles as a writer who confined himself to the problems of Greek man. *τοῦτο τὸ δρᾶμα* [i.e. *Rhesus*] *ἔνιοι νόθον ὑπενόησαν ὡς οὐκ ὂν Εὐριπίδου· τὸν γὰρ Σοφόκλειον μᾶλλον ὑποφαίνειν χαρακτῆρα.* Certainly a play so full of exotic effects would not be described as "Sophoclean" unless Sophocles were known to use such effects in other plays. Exclamations of horror at this suggestion of the ancient critic (e.g., W. N. Bates, *Euripides, a Student of Human Nature* [Philadelphia, 1930], p. 190) are perhaps due to the conventional misconception of Sophocles as "pure Greek." Pearson ("The *Rhesus*," p. 60) observes, "No one has ventured to attribute the play to him [i.e., Sophocles], but the remark should not be scouted as merely perverse." He sees the Sophoclean element in the close adherence to Homeric plot and characterization. I am suggesting that still another Sophoclean (and highly un-Homeric) note is the realistic treatment of Thracian dress, behavior, religion, etc. Wilamowitz (*Einleitung in die attische Tragödie*, p. 41, n. 81) says *Rhesus* has Sophoclean characteristics, but does not illustrate.

The influence of Herodotus shows itself most strongly in the richness of the references to foreign words and customs. Sophocles has more, and more varied, information on these points than Aeschylus has. As we have seen, a great many of the words and customs are actually referred to by Herodotus. This catholic kind of interest in men and manners from Scythia to Italy is, of course, quite typical of the historian, though Herodotus would never have violated history by representing Trojans and Phrygians as Persians. The context of these references shows that on the whole they are not digressions, like the reference to Egyptian custom in *Oedipus at Colonus*, but were used in many of the lost plays to create a realistic foreign setting, or to give reality to foreign characters. Just how far and how consistently he pursued this practice we cannot know, unless we can dig up some of the lost foreign plays; but the fact that foreign words are used in dialogue as well as lyric suggests that in some cases foreignness was a basic part of characterization. If the detailed and meticulous treatment of Trojans as Persians, and the concreteness of some of his other information, are valid evidence for his general approach, we can guess that his foreign scenes and characters were as detailed and vivid and effective as those of Aeschylus, and possibly a little more accurate.

4. EURIPIDES

Language

Ten passages of Euripides refer to the peculiarities of foreign speech. All of them are from the extant plays, and most of them seem to involve music as well as words. The companions of Iphigenia may be thinking of music as much as words when they sing (*IT* 179–81)

> ἀντιψάλμους ᾠδὰς ὕμνων τ'
> Ἀσιητᾶν σοι βάρβαρον ἀχὰν
> δεσποίνᾳ γ' ἐξαυδάσω.

In the famous opening ode of *Bacchae* the reference may be as much to music as to speech (*Bacch.* 158–9).

> εὔια τὸν εὔιον ἀγαλλόμεναι θεὸν
> ἐν Φρυγίαισι βοαῖς ἐνοπαῖσί τε.

When the chorus of *Bacchae* greets the news of Pentheus' death (*Bacch.* 1034),

> εὐάζω ξένα μέλεσι βαρβάροις,

the reference to music is definite, though it is not certain whether it is the tune or the words, or both, that are *βάρβαρα*. The words *ξένα* and *βαρβάροις* emphasize the foreignness of the chorus. One naturally infers that their speech as well as their song is foreign. The Phrygian slave of *Orestes* mourns for Troy in his own tongue (*Or.* 1384–5 and 1395–7),

> *ὥς σ' ὀλόμενον στένω*
> *[ἁρμάτειον ἁρμάτειον μέλος],*
> *βαρβάρῳ βοᾷ . . .*
> *αἴλινον αἴλινον ἀρχὰν θανάτου*
> *βάρβαροι λέγουσιν, αἰαῖ,*
> *Ἀσιάδι φωνᾷ.*

The Phrygian also speaks of the songs he sang to Helen as he fanned her, calling them once *Φρύγιοι νόμοι* and once *βάρβαροι νόμοι* (*Or.* 1426–30). It is natural to assume that he refers to words as well as music. In *Phoenissae* Jocasta tells the chorus she has come because she has heard their *Φοίνισσα βοά* (*Phoen.* 301). The chorus of this play three times refer to their own foreign way of speaking. They call on Cadmus and his forbears to help Thebes (*Phoen.* 678–80),

> *Ἔπαφον, ὦ Διὸς γένεθλον,*
> *[ἐκάλεσ'] ἐκάλεσα βαρβάρῳ βοᾷ,*
> *ἰώ, βαρβάροις λιταῖς.*

They speak of hearing the story of the origin of the Spartoi told them in their home in Phoenicia (*Phoen.* 819),

> *βάρβαρον ὡς ἀκοὰν ἐδάην ἐδάην ποτ' ἐν οἴκοις.*

The story is *βάρβαρος*, I suppose, because it was told in a foreign tongue. They will mourn for Eteocles and Polyneices *βοᾷ βαρβάρῳ* (*Phoen.* 1301).

Of actual foreign words Euripides uses only six (compare Aeschylus' 22 and Sophocles' 20). Only one of these comes from the fragments.

αἴλινον (*HF* 348; *Helen* 172; *Phoen.* 1519; *Or.* 1395; also used by Aeschylus, see p. 22, above). Only in *Orestes* and *Phoenissae* are its foreign overtones appropriate. In the other passages it is a conventional word of sorrow spoken by Greeks (cf. *Ag.* 121, etc.).

βᾶρις, a boat (*IA* 297; also used by Aeschylus, see above, p. 20). The women of Chalcis call the Trojan ships *βάρβαροι βάριδες*, as though to emphasize their outlandishness.

βύσσινος, an adjective for fine linen or cotton (*Bacch.* 821; also used by Aeschylus; see p. 21, above).

μάγος, a priest, often a priestly impostor (*Or.* 1498; also used by Sophocles, see above, p. 67).

μίτρα, an oriental headdress is used five times (*El.* 163; *Bacch.* 833, 929, 1115; *Hec.* 924; also used by Aeschylus; see above, p. 22, and below, pp. 123–4 and n. 2).

παρασάγγης, presumably the Persian measure of distance (fr. 686 *Scyrii;* also used by Sophocles, but with a special meaning; see above, p. 69).

Gorgeously cacophonous passages like those of Aeschylus do not occur in Euripides. An occasional phrase like *βάρβαρος βοά* may be intended to have this effect. It is possible that a systematic study might reveal that he uses certain lyric meters specifically to convey the idea of foreigners speaking in a strange tongue.[1]

There is some suggestion of foreignness in the language of the choruses of *Bacchae* and *Phoenissae*, of the Taurians in *Iphigenia Among the Taurians*, of the Egyptians in *Helen*—more by implication than by any specific dramatic indication—and of the Phrygian eunuch in *Orestes*. He is the only character of Trojan origin in Euripides who is represented as speaking or acting in a foreign manner. In the eight plays that deal more or less directly with the Trojan story Euripides makes no other reference to a difference in language. The treatment of the Phrygian, in its repeated reference to language, and in the excitement of its rhythms, can be compared to the treatment of Aeschylus' Cassandra; in its emphasis on Persian qualities, linguistic and other (see below, pp. 124, 146–7), it can be compared to Sophocles' treatment of Trojans in some of

1. On Euripides' foreign vocabulary, and references to foreign speech, almost nothing has been written. Krausse (*De Euripide Aeschyli instauratore*, p. 208), who compares the vocabulary of Aeschylus and Euripides in great detail, points out that Euripides differs from his two predecessors in avoiding the use of strange and obsolete words as a way of indicating foreign nationality, and suggests that he relied on music for his foreign effects. This is the only discussion of the subject I have found.

the lost plays. More significant, I think, than the emphasis of this one scene is the omission of all, or almost all, reference to foreign speech in so many places where it would not be out of place—namely, in the case of *all* the other Trojan characters, of the Egyptians in *Helen,* of Thoas and the messengers in *Iphigenia Among the Taurians*, of Dionysus, of Medea even in her most extreme homesickness.

All the passages that contain foreign words or refer to foreign speech are lyric. Though there are many foreign characters in Euripides' plays, nowhere is there any attempt to give a foreign cast to their speech in a dialogue passage, as Aeschylus does with Cassandra, with the Danaids, and with his Persian characters, and as Sophocles did in some of the lost plays. Euripides' foreign characters use neither foreign words nor foreign expressions. His references to foreign speech are not basically characterizations as Aeschylus' are. They are isolated in lyric passages, and they are fairly consistently all of one kind. They all contain a reference to mourning or to song, or to both. Three of the ten references use the phrase *βαρβάρῳ βοᾷ*, two others the variants *Φρυγίαισι βοαῖς*, and *Φοίνισσαν βοάν*. As I have already suggested, here if anywhere he attempts to suggest foreign speech through onomatopoeia. The repetition of this formula with minor variations indicates that it is a conventional device for giving an exotic flavor to certain lyrics, particularly of the tearful variety—a bit of incidental color, rather than an essential part of a character or an action. It lacks any reference to a particular nationality, and will do equally well for Lydian, Phoenician, or Trojan; and nothing else in the context—except in the case of the Phrygian—makes the reference less vague. Aeschylus' references—and I think we may assume Sophocles' too—assert and explain a fact about a foreign character. Foreign speech is part of Aeschylus' characterization and part of the structure of his plays. He is careful to establish and emphasize this detail in order to make a convincing, often realistic, foreign character.

In Euripides' fragments the only reference of any kind to foreign language is the single word *παρασάγγης* in *Scyrii*. From this we may guess that in this respect the method of the lost plays did not differ from that of the extant ones. Presumably references to foreign speech, if any, were so vague and so formulaic as not to be worth quoting. It is unlikely, if Euripides had used curious foreign words as Aeschylus and Sophocles did, that theirs should have been quoted and not his.

In contrast to Aeschylus and Sophocles, then, Euripides pays comparatively little attention to the language of his foreign characters. His occasional references all occur in lyric passages. They tend to be formulaic and designed to create a vague sense of the exotic rather than to create a consistent characterization of a specific national type.

Physical appearance

This is a subject barely noticed by Euripides, which is more surprising in his case than in the case of Sophocles, since so many of the extant plays contain foreign characters in open conflict with Greeks.

The long hair and pale skin of Dionysus in *Bacchae* (453–9) seem to me as much the result of an effeminate way of life as an inherent physical difference.

A visible physical difference between Greeks and Taurians is perhaps implied in *Iphigenia Among the Taurians* (72–3). Pylades and Orestes have just noticed the sacrificial altar of the Tauric Artemis.

> Ορ. καὶ βωμός, Ἕλλην οὗ καταστάζει φόνος;
> Πυ. ἐξ αἱμάτων γοῦν ξάνθ' ἔχει τριχώματα.

In *Phaethon* (fr. 771) we meet the γείτονες μελάμβροτοι of Merops. These seem to be eastern Ethiopians, since Merops lives in the region of the rising sun.

If Euripides neglects this topic it must be because he feels it is not dramatically relevant, since play after play (e.g. *Helen*, *IT*, *Phoen.*, *Medea*, and all the Trojan plays) afforded him the opportunity to refer to it and develop it even more extensively than Aeschylus did in *Suppliants*. Looking different is not, for him, an essential part of the characterization of foreigners, any more than speaking differently is.

Costume

Euripides' references to foreign costume are of two kinds. There is the vague description of something simply different and more luxurious, and the mention of some specific article or style of foreign dress. They are about equal in number, and all of them come from the extant plays. Even the most specific of them lack the richness of detail and the concreteness we have found in Aeschylus and Sophocles. And, considering the number of extant plays, and the quantity of the fragments, the number of such references, 12, not counting the repetitions of the word *μίτρα* in *Bacchae* (see above, p. 117), as compared with Aeschylus' 15, out of seven plays and the fragments, and Sophocles' 7, from the fragments alone, is not very great.

The following belong in the category of vague description. All but the first three passages take richness as the principal characteristic of barbarian costume. When Demophon describes the Argive herald, he only indicates that foreign dress is different from Greek (*Heracl.* 130–1).

> καὶ μὴν στολήν γ' Ἕλληνα καὶ ῥυθμὸν πέπλων
> ἔχει, τὰ δ' ἔργα βαρβάρου χερὸς τάδε.

Agamemnon speaking of the dead Polydorus again tells us nothing about the *kind* of clothes on the body, but only that they look different (*Hec.* 734–5).

> οὐ γὰρ Ἀργεῖον πέπλοι
> δέμας περιπτύσσοντες ἀγγέλλουσί μοι.

Polymestor's description of the Trojan women pretending to admire his foreign clothes contains no concrete information (*Hec.* 1153–4).

> κερκίδ' Ἠδώνης χερὸς
> ᾔνουν ὑπ' αὐγὰς τούσδε λεύσσουσαι πέπλους.

In the four passages that follow, the only distinguishing characteristic of Trojan dress is its richness. Hecuba describes Paris when Helen first saw him (*Tro.* 991–2) as

> βαρβάροις ἐσθήμασι
> χρυσῷ τε λαμπρόν.

She speaks of the robes in which she wraps the body of Astyanax (*Tro.* 1218–20).

> ἃ δ' ἐν γάμοισι χρῆν σε προσθέσθαι χροῒ
> Ἀσιατίδων γήμαντα τὴν ὑπερτάτην
> Φρύγια πέπλων ἀγάλματ'.

Electra describes the Trojan captives who serve Clytemnestra (*El.* 317–8),

> Ἰδαῖα φάρη χρυσέαις ἐζευγμέναι
> πόρπαισιν.

Agamemnon describes Paris (*IA* 73–4),

> ἀνθηρὸς μὲν εἱμάτων στολῇ
> χρυσῷ δὲ λαμπρός, βαρβάρῳ χλιδήματι.

The reference to wealth is so frequent as to be formulaic in effect. It creates a general atmosphere of richness and strangeness without any precise concrete detail.

The references that follow are a little more specific. The μίτρα, mentioned five times, is at least an identifiable article of dress with slightly foreign associations.[2] The Phrygian slave wears the same kind of shoe (εὔμαρις *Or.* 1370) as Aeschylus' Darius (*Pers.* 660, see above, p. 28). But Aeschylus, typically, tells the color of Darius' shoes—saffron—and Gow refers to a Persian monument that substantiates him.[3] The burlesque version of Helen's first view of Paris is more specific than the tragic one (*Cyc.* 182–4).

> ἣ τοὺς θυλάκους τοὺς ποικίλους
> περὶ τοῖν σκελοῖν ἰδοῦσα καὶ τὸν χρύσεον
> κλῳὸν φοροῦντα περὶ μεσὸν τὸν αὐχένα
> ἐξεπτοήθη.

He wears gaudy trousers and a gold collar. The Trojan is again figuring as a Persian. Is Euripides referring to a genuine article of Persian dress, or to those gaily decorated longsleeved leotards—the conventional dress of

2. We may assume that the μίτρα referred to in all these passages is the many-colored headband often seen on representations of Dionysus and his followers, both male and female. Like the Ionian chiton it was prevalent in Greece but regarded as an Eastern style. From this it came to be used of various types of oriental diadem including the τιάρα (see Schuppe in PW, *15*, 2218–20, s.v., and A. DeRidder in Darem.-Sag., *3*, 1955–6, s.v.). None of the derived meanings fits the context of the Euripidean passages so well as the original. In *Bacchae* the reference is obviously to the Dionysiac headband. In *Electra* (163) οὐ μίτραισι γυνή σε δέξατ' (Seidler for οὐ μίτραις σε γυνή), it seems to be a victor's fillet (see Paley [*Euripides, with an English Commentary* (2nd ed. 3 vols. London 1872–8)] ad loc.). In *Hecuba* (924) ἐγὼ δὲ πλόκαμον ἀναδέτοις μίτραισιν ἐρρυθμιζόμαν, it is clearly a band for binding the hair.

3. "Notes on the *Persae*," p. 148. See also above, p. 28, n. 13.

barbarians, regardless of nationality, in Greek vase painting?[4]

In his description of how Polyxena bared her breast to the knife (*Hec.* 558–61), Euripides must be thinking of the Ionian chiton rather than the Doric peplos. The Doric peplos, pinned on the shoulders and open on one side, would not have to be torn from collar bone to navel to expose the breast. In fact it would be difficult and unnecessary to tear it because it is double above the waist, and would fall to the waist without tearing when the pins were removed (see above, p. 27 with n. 12).[5] The Ionian chiton was not, however, an exclusively Asiatic form of dress, and Euripides does not give any specifically foreign details to Polyxena's gown. Though it is not the traditional dress of the Dorian maiden, it is a costume that might be worn by an Athenian lady of fashion.

The chorus of *Hecuba* describe how they leapt from their beds when they discovered the Greeks were sacking Troy (*Hec.* 933–4).

λέχη δὲ φίλια μονόπεπλος
λιποῦσα Δωρὶς ὣς κόρα . . .

4. θύλακοι, apparently a slang word for Persian ἀναξυρίδες (schol. in Aristophanes, *Wasps* 1087). The root meaning of the word is "sack," from which E. Saglio infers (Darem.-Sag., *1*, 746, s.v. *Bracae*) that they were loose trousers rather than the close-fitting garments of vase paintings. For the gold collars of the Persians see Hdt. 3.20; 9.80; for the trousers 5.49, 7.61.

5. I give the same general interpretation of Polyxena's dress as Studniczka ("Beiträge zur Geschichte der altgriechischen Tracht," p. 28).

Again the contrast seems to be between the Doric peplos and the more complicated arrangements of chiton and himation worn in Ionia and Asia. But, as I have said, this form of dress was used in Greece too. No specifically foreign type of costume is mentioned. The preceding description of the Trojan lady's undressing (923–7) is not, except for the reference to the mitra, foreign in tone. And even the mitra was naturalized in Greece (see above, p. 124 with n. 2). The graceful scene of the lady doing her hair before her mirror belongs on a red figured vase or white ground lekythos. It is all Greek. These two passages scarcely deserve to be classified as references to foreign dress. They only suggest that Trojan women did not follow the strictest conventions of Dorian dress.

When repetitions are counted, Euripides has not 12 but 16 references to foreign dress. Of these the only identifiably foreign objects are the *μίτρα*, the *εὔμαρις*, and Paris's trousers and gold collar. All the plays and fragments of Euripides can produce only these four things. This is in great contrast to the wealth of material in Aeschylus, or even to the few but specific words from Sophocles' fragments—*σάρητον*, *τιάρα*, *σίσυρα*, *ψέλια*.

And yet the number of references—in comparison with the amount of information—in Euripides is high. But like other kinds of references they are usually vague and formulaic—for example, his habit of referring to Trojan costume as rich, without further description. The number of repetitions of mitra, and the lack of other words of this type, suggests that it is a stock article used by Euripides as a conventional way of referring to foreign attire. He wishes to suggest that his foreign characters look different, but unlike Aeschylus and Sophocles, he does not bother to tell us specifically how. Whether or not his costume designer tried to make up for this omission is something we are not in a position to know.

Objects

Euripides has a large number of conventional passing references to foreign objects, all but one of them in the extant plays. Information of the kind we find in Sophocles' fragments is almost entirely lacking.

Certain musical instruments are foreign more by poetic convention than for any necessity of the context; the Tyrrhenian trumpet (*Heracl.* 830; *Phoen.* 1377; see above, pp. 32 and 76), the Asiatic cithara (*Cyc.* 443), the Libyan flute (*Alc.* 346; *HF* 684; *Tro.* 544; *Helen* 170; *IA* 1036), the Phrygian tympanum (*Bacch.* 58), the Phrygian flute (*Bacch.* 127; *IA* 576). In all these passages the foreign epithet is conventional —i.e., irrelevant to the subject matter—except in the case of the tympanum and flute of *Bacchae,* whose Phrygian origin is stressed because of their connections with the cult of Rhea. Contrast Sophocles' assortment of instruments with genuinely foreign names (above, pp. 76–7).

"Thracian" when applied to shields (*Alc.* 498; *Hec.*

1155; fr. 369 *Erechtheus*) is again an epithet rather than a description. The Thracian shields of the *Erechtheus* fragment are the only foreign objects mentioned in the fragments. In the same spirit, the ships of Egypt are Sidonian (*Helen* 1413, 1451, 1531), Orphic books are called Thracian tablets (*Alc.* 967), ship cables—made of byblus—are called πλεκτὰν Αἰγύπτου παιδείαν (*Tro.* 128), Ion serves wine of Byblus (*Ion* 1195).

In connection with foreign things a generalized effect of wealth and luxury is more usual than specific information. In the boudoir scene described by the chorus of *Hecuba* the lady does her hair before a golden mirror (*Hec.* 925–6). Perhaps the gold is meant to give a note of Eastern luxury.[6] The myrrh and mirrors brought from Troy by Helen are called τρυφὰς . . . Τρωικάς (*Or.* 1113).

When Antigone questions the old tutor about the Aetolian Tydeus, recognizably foreign weapons are referred to (*Phoen.* 138–40).[7]

6. χρυσέων ἐνόπτρων λεύσσουσ' ἀτέρμονας εἰς αὐγάς. N. E. Collinge suggests in an ingenious note ("Euripides' *Hecuba* 925–6," *Classical Philology* 49 [1954], 35–6) that ἀτέρμονας εἰς αὐγάς means that the lady was contemplating an endless series of reflections produced by using *two* mirrors, another sign of Trojan luxury.

7. For the semi-barbarous character sometimes attributed to Aetolians see above, p. 32 with n. 15 and p. 36. As a general rule I have not treated Meleager, Althea, and other figures of the Aetolian story as barbarians. They seem to belong in the Greek tradition even more firmly than the Argive kings of Macedon. Nothing in the myths indicates that they are barbarians. The character of Tydeus in *Seven* and *Phoenissae*

Αν. . . . ὡς ἀλλόχρως, ὅπλοισι μειξοβάβαρος.
Πα. σακέσφοροι γὰρ πάντες Αἰτωλοί, τέκνον,
λόγχαις τ' ἀκοντιστῆρες εὐστοχώτατοι.

The Phrygian eunuch fans Helen εὐπαγεῖ κύκλῳ πτερίνῳ (*Or.* 1426–30). A round feather fan in the hands of a eunuch is a definitely exotic touch.

Of the twenty-four references just cited only the last two are detailed and concrete enough to give a clear picture of a specifically foreign object. The other twenty-two create a vague impression of something foreign by the use of an ethnic or geographical adjective, or a reference to wealth.

Art and architecture

There is little in the plays of Aeschylus and Sophocles to guide the scene designer. Aeschylus passes up even very obvious opportunities. Of the tomb of Darius and the carpet on which Agamemnon paced shoeless to his downfall the poet tells us almost nothing. Euripides, on the other hand, goes out of his way to refer to and describe objects of art and architecture. Some of these are in foreign lands, or of foreign origin, and can afford us further evidence about Euripides' handling of foreign material.[8]

---

is probably to be attributed not to mythology, but to Athenian experience of Aetolians in the 5th century.

8. From his study of references to art and architecture in the tragedians, Miller (*Daedalus and Thespis*, *1*, 20) concludes that (1) Sophocles has the fewest and the vaguest

The hangings with which Ion decorates his festival tent are described in great detail (*Ion* 1143–62). The scene, to be sure, is Delphi, but Euripides represents the hangings as foreign spoil captured by Heracles from the Amazons, and indicates that both the work and the subject matter are barbarian. The following scenes are represented—Uranus marshalling the stars in the circle of the ether, while Helius drives his horses to their setting and brings after him the light of Hesperus; Night with her chariot followed by stars (Pleiades, Orion, and the Bear, the Moon, the Hyades) and Eos pursuing the stars; ships fighting Greek ships; half beast men; deer hunts on horseback; lion hunts. There is nothing here that could not have occurred in a Greek work of art. The names of the gods are all familiar from Greek mythology. The hunting scenes and *μειξόθηρες φῶτες* can be thought of as oriental, but they also occur in Greek art from Mycenaean times on, and they are not given a specifically foreign character here.[9] The richness and diversity of the hangings

---

references (242 in all, including fragments), and mentions contemporary art only in connection with Colonus; (2) Aeschylus never refers to contemporary art (this is in keeping with the realism which I have pointed out in other connections); (3) Euripides has by far the largest number of references (892), many of them to contemporary works of art or architecture like the Apollo temple at Delphi. This disregard of chronology is another sign of that lack of concern for technical accuracy which appears in his treatment of foreign material.

9. A. S. Owen in his edition of *Ion* (Oxford, 1939, ad loc.) regards the scenes as oriental. Some justification for this may

is perhaps meant to suggest barbarian workmanship, but we know from the descriptions of Athene's peplos that Greeks also did work of this kind.[10] Euripides apparently did not feel that it was necessary to make the hangings realistically foreign.

---

be found in *Frogs* 937–8, where Euripides defending his art to Aeschylus says,

> οὐχ ἱππαλεκτρυόνας μὰ Δί' οὐδὲ τραγελάφους, ἅπερ σύ,
> ἂν τοῖσι παραπετάσμασιν τοῖς Μηδικοῖς γράφουσιν.

Alföldi ("Gewaltherrscher und Theaterkönig," p. 32) also assumes the hangings are Persian, and suggests that the tent is modelled on actual tents captured from the Persians at Plataea. He gives no reasons for regarding the scenes or the hangings as more Persian than Greek. The display of wealth in all the appointments of the feast implies barbarism to him. See above, p. 29, n. 13. On the other hand Wilamowitz commenting on lines 1144 and 1159 in his edition of *Ion* (Berlin, 1926) points out that the workmanship of the hangings may be foreign but the subjects are all common to Greek vase painting. The μειξόθηρες φῶτες, he suggests, are centaurs. Similar representations of sun, moon, stars, dawn, etc. are too familiar to need detailed illustration. I need only refer to the east pediment of the Parthenon, a black figured lekythos in the Metropolitan bearing figures labelled Νύξ, Ἠώς, and Ἥλιος (accession nos. 41, 62, 29, illustrated in G. M. A. Richter, *Greek Painting, The Metropolitan Museum of Art* [4th ed. New York, 1952], p. 10), and the Blacas vase in the British Museum. Miller (*Daedalus and Thespis, 3*, 667) observes the parallel with the Blacas vase, but also suggests (*3*, 668) that Euripides may have been describing a genuine work of the famous weaver Helicon of Cyprus. It seems unlikely that the tapestry is at the same time an oriental work of art and a companion piece to the Blacas vase.

10. Miller, *Daedalus and Thespis, 2*, 651–4, *3*, 673–4. The most detailed descriptions of the πέπλος are by Euripides himself, *Hec.* 466–74 and *IT* 222–4.

The temple of Tauric Artemis is referred to frequently and quite specifically. Here, if anywhere, we might expect a touch of barbarian local color. But on the contrary we find that most of the words applied to it are the same as those applied to the temple of Apollo at Delphi in *Ion*. Euripides thinks of them both in the same category of traditional large-scale Doric temples. The only important difference is that Euripides mentions no sculpture in connection with the Tauric temple. His description of the sculptures at Delphi of course is famous (*Ion* 184–218).[11] It is something of a surprise to find that the temple of this savage cult among the natives of south Russia is neither outlandishly splendid nor crudely primitive, but a traditional Greek building of fairly imposing proportions.

Orestes and Pylades, discussing the building and how to get into it in order to carry off the cult image, tell us a good deal about it. From the fact that it has triglyphs we may infer that it is Doric (*IT* 113–14).

> ὅρα δέ γ' εἴσω τριγλύφων ὅποι κενὸν
> δέμας καθεῖναι.

11. Archaeological finds make it fairly certain that Euripides is describing the actual pediments of the 6th century Alcmaeonid temple. See Miller, *Daedalus and Thespis, 1*, 45–56. Dumping a late 6th century building into a story about Athens in the days of the kings is a sign of that independence of the realities of time and place which is typical of Euripides. In this passage the conscious blending of the real and the impossible has perhaps some of the piquant quality of Alexandrian art, e.g., the scenes on the wooden bowl in Theocritus *Idyl* 1.

It is no small affair *in antis*, but peripteral, if περικίονας can be taken in what would seem to be its natural sense (*IT* 402–6).[12]

12. My reconstruction in most respects agrees with Miller's (*Daedalus and Thespis, 1*, 105 ff), except that he argues for a temple *in antis* on the basis of 1159, ἄναξ, ἔχ' αὐτοῦ πόδα σὸν ἐν παραστάσιν. From the presence of *antae* (παραστάς) he infers that there is no peristyle and therefore concludes that περκίονας is not to be taken literally but as an "*epitheton ornans*" (ibid., p. 106). Besides making nonsense of περικίων (406) and εὔστυλος (129), this interpretation also assumes that peripteral temples do not have *antae*, which is not true. But it is not necessary to go into technicalities, since Euripides himself refers to a παραστάς of the Apollo temple in Delphi (*Andr.* 1121. Or are we to assume that the temple in *Andromache* is more primitive than that in *Ion?*). Perhaps a stronger argument for a temple *in antis* is based on Pylades' suggestion that the temple can be entered εἴσω τριγλύφων ὅποι κενὸν δέμας καθεῖναι (113–14; cf. the Phrygian's means of escape from the palace in Mycenae, *Or.* 1371–2, κεδρωτὰ παστάδων ὑπὲρ τέραμνα Δωρικάς τε τριγλύφους). Miller (ibid., 110–17) maintains that this proves (1) that the metopes were empty, therefore without sculpture, and (2) that the temple was *in antis*, otherwise going through the frieze would only bring Orestes and Pylades inside the colonnade. But he does not dispose of the argument that they might have gotten into the attic behind the frieze and thence into the *cella*. If open metopes are a sign of primitivism then Agamemnon's palace in Mycenae is also primitive. Miller argues that a temple *in antis*, without sculpture, with doors of wood instead of bronze, indicates primitive simplicity appropriate to the Taurians. The absence of sculpture and colonnade seem to me not proved, but if they were, such simplicity as they suggest is still not barbarian, but Greek. The temple, though the home of a barbarian cult in a foreign land, is thoroughly Doric in architecture. There is no doubt that the note of ad-

. . . ἔνθα κούρᾳ
δίᾳ τέγγει
βωμοὺς καὶ περικίονας
ναοὺς αἷμα βρότειον.

The doors are massive. Orestes and Pylades almost despair of springing their brass bolts with crowbars (*IT* 99),

χαλκότευκτα κλῇθρα λύσαντες μοχλοῖς.

The doors are well dowelled, εὐγόμφους, therefore of wood, not bronze (*IT* 1286).[13] At least the lower part of the temple is of stone, since stone bases must rest on stone floors (*IT* 996–7).

ἡνίκ᾽ ἂν κενὰς
κρηπῖδας εὕρῃ λαΐνας ἀγάλματος.

It has high walls (*IT* 96–7),[14]

ἀμφίβληστρα γὰρ τοίχων ὁρᾷς
ὑψηλά.

It has fine columns, and gilt or gold coping stones (*IT* 129).

εὐστύλων
ναῶν χρυσήρεις θριγκούς.

---

miring wonder for Apollo's house which occurs throughout *Ion* is missing in *IT*. But this is as far as Euripides goes in suggesting primitivism.

13. Miller, *Daedalus and Thespis, 1*, 106–7.

14. Ibid., p. 111.

Like any Greek temple it has an altar in front. Orestes and Pylades and the chorus see it, stained with human blood, as they enter (*IT* 402–6 and 72–5). Inside is the cult statue (*IT* 113–14),

> τολμητέον τοι ξεστὸν ἐκ ναοῦ λαβεῖν
> ἄγαλμα πάσας προσφέροντε μηχανάς.

There is probably a second altar inside, as at Delphi, since the actual sacrifice was performed inside the temple (*IT* 725–6).[15] The statue itself is perhaps the only primitive thing about the temple. It must be thought of as small and wooden, since Iphigenia appears on stage carrying it in her arms (*IT* 1044–5, 1157–8),[16] but we have seen that it stood on a stone base. Primitive, however, is not foreign. Such crude statues, sanctified by age and ritual, are not uncommon in Greek cult.[17]

Most of the architectural words in these quotations are also used in *Ion* of the temple of Apollo at Delphi —δόμοι,[18] κρηπῖδες, ναός, θριγκοί, χρυσήρης, εὔστυλοι (*Ion* has εὐκίονες) λάϊνος, πυλοί, μέλαθρα. Ion's remark to the troublesome birds (*Ion* 156–7),

> αὐδῶ μὴ χρίμπτειν θριγκοῖς
> μηδ' ἐς χρυσήρεις οἴκους—

15. Ibid., p. 108.
16. Ibid., pp. 117–19.
17. Ibid., p. 344.
18. Miller in another discussion (ibid., p. 45 with n. 1) regards the use of δόμοι as itself an indication of size. He instances *Eum.* 577–8 and 669, where it is used of the Apollo

seems to refer to the same part of the building, and in similar language, as one of the lines just quoted (*IT* 129),[19]

εὐστύλων ναῶν χρυσήρεις θρίγκους.

Such terms as these, unless qualified by some suggestion of strangeness, could only remind a Greek audience of their own architecture.[20]

There is just one touch of outlandishness. When Orestes and Pylades first come on the temple, this dialogue takes place (*IT* 72–5).

Ορ. καὶ βωμός, Ἕλλην οὗ καταστάζει φόνος;
Πυ. ἐξ αἱμάτων γοῦν ξάνθ' ἔχει τριχώματα.
Ορ. θριγκοῖς δ' ὑπ' αὐτοῖς σκῦλ' ὁρᾷς ἠρτημένα;
Πυ. τῶν κατθανόντων γ' ἀκροθίνια ξένων.

One certainly would not expect to see human blood and hair (how did they know it was human?) on a

temple in Delphi and the old Athene temple on the Acropolis, and suggests that it refers to a multiplicity of rooms.

19. Miller (ibid., p. 60) compares these two passages and concludes that the passage in *IT* proves that the passage in *Ion* refers to exterior gold decoration. Here he seems to take it for granted that the Tauric temple is in the same style as the Delphic one, though less magnificent.

20. Some of the more important references to the architecture of the two buildings are *IT* 69, 72, 74, 86–8, 96–101, 113, 128–9, 159–69, 405, 995–7, 1040, 1079, 1155 ff, 1201, 1214–16, 1222, 1286–7, 1294, 1304–10, and *Ion* 33–4, 38–9, 45–9, 55, 79, 97, 114, 129–30, 156–7, 172–3, 177, 185–6, 206–7, 220, 226–8, 233, 514–6, 738, 974, 1224, 1255, 1275, 1280, 1306, 1309, 1373, 1403, 1547–50.

Greek altar, or the spoils of the victims (skulls?) hung up under the coping stones.[21] But we know that the architrave was a traditional place for displaying spoil on a Greek temple.[22]

Euripides mentions a few other foreign temples—in Troy (*Hec.* 935–6, 1008–10; *Tro.* 25, 308–10, 539–41, 1060–4), in Egypt (*Alc.* 116–19; *El.* 734–6), in Leuke Akte (*Andr.* 117–19). These are as completely without detailed description as the sacked shrines of Troy in *Agamemnon.*[23]

In *Helen* the palace of Theoclymenus and the tomb of Proteus, like the tomb and palace of Darius in *Persae*, are referred to without any attempt to distinguish them from Greek buildings. The palace is simply εὔθριγκος and rich. It is compared to the house of Plutus (*Helen* 68–70, 430–4). There is, perhaps, an ironic touch here, since it is in fact a house of death

21. Even this need not be thought of as an exclusively barbarian practice, since Sophocles had Oenomaus display the skulls of Hippodamia's suitors in a similar fashion (see above, p. 78, n. 16, and schol. Pindar, *Olympian* 1.79). Other mythological characters who committed this type of outrage were the Thracian Diomedes, Antaeus, and Evenus the father of Marpessa (schol. Pindar, *Isthmian* 3.92 [4.54]). The first two are barbarians; Evenus is an Aetolian.

22. According to Aeschines (*Against Ctesiphon* 115 ff) the Athenians hung shields taken from the Thebans at Plataea on the architrave of the Apollo temple at Delphi (cf. Miller, *Daedalus and Thespis*, *1*, 59). Miller (ibid., p. 109) thinks the spoil is displayed on the cornice of the altar, rather than the temple.

23. These temples are discussed by Miller, ibid., pp. 193–6.

(Πλούτων) as well as a house of wealth (Πλοῦτος), for Greeks; but nothing specific is said of its appearance. The tomb of Proteus is described in the same terms as the tombs of Agamemnon (*Cho.* 306–509), Antigone (*Ant.* 1204–18), Phaethon (fr. 781, 8–10), Achilles (*Hec.* 521–4), which can all be made to fit the pattern of the tholos.[24] Like most Greek buildings it has a

24. Miller, ibid., pp. 236–9. The language in *Helen* is too vague to make definite conclusions possible, but the following facts favor Miller's interpretation. The tomb is the stone underground home of Proteus (*Helen* 61–2, 961–8), a building where Helen can take sanctuary (*Helen* 797–800), a tomb on whose "back" (τύμβου 'πι νώτοις τοῦδ') Menelaus can plan to kill Helen and himself (*Helen* 984). The word ξεστός applied to it in 986 is used generally of Mycenaean stone work, and particularly of tombs (Miller, ibid., pp. 235–9). But whether or not it is a θόλος tomb it is clearly like other tombs of Greek drama with a mound on top where offerings can be laid and people can stand, and an underground chamber where not only the body but also the spirit (since Proteus is invoked directly in 962–8) is in some sense present. Cf. the invocation of Darius (*Pers.* 623–80), of Agamemnon (*Cho.* 306–509); Antigone's tomb, which involves an underground stone chamber with something like a dromos (χῶμα) from which stones are removed to make an entrance (*Ant.* 1204–18); the use of ὄχθος (a mound or slope) to describe the tombs of Agamemnon (*Cho.* 4), Darius (*Pers.* 659), and the Danaids (*Eur.*, fr. 305 *Bellerophon*). There is some uncertainty about the last reference, which may be to a palace rather than a tomb. If Aeschylus represented the tombs of Agamemnon and Darius as similar he probably did so out of ignorance rather than carelessness. We have seen that in general he was carefully realistic in representing foreign matters. There is nothing in the description of the combina-

κρηπίς and ὀρθοστάται (*Helen* 546). Nothing suggests that its style is foreign.

Hecuba and *Troiades*, being laid in a foreign country, also provide opportunities to develop a foreign atmosphere by references to the art and architecture of the setting. But there are only generalized descriptions of Troy, burning or in ashes—descriptions which, except for a tendency to dwell on the wealth of the captured city, might just as well be applied to a Greek as to a barbarian city. From *Ion* and *Bacchae* we know Euripides' gift for describing landscape and buildings. If then we find him neglecting the settings of his foreign plays, we can be sure he does so from lack of interest, not lack of skill.

Like Euripides, Aeschylus and Sophocles sometimes pass up opportunities to refer to the exotic "properties" in a foreign setting. *Persae* and *Ajax* are examples of this. But we have no evidence that would lead us to suppose that either of them was as flagrantly unrealistic as Euripides in describing foreign objects as though they were Greek. As usual it is Euripides who shows the least concern with the realistic detail of the foreign environment. When he wishes to indicate foreign atmosphere he does it, not through concrete information,

---

tion treasure house and tomb in *Phaethon* (Eur., fr. 781) that would indicate that it is different from the buildings just discussed (see Miller, ibid., p. 238). This is consistent with the shimmer of romance and unreality in the fragments of this play, which avoids specifically foreign details.

but with a few vague formulae about the savagery of the Taurians, and the wealth of Troy, Egypt, and the kingdom of Merops.

Religion, customs, manners

Foreign religions are important in Euripides' plays, but concrete information about them is relatively scarce. Imagine a *Bacchae* of Aeschylus. The fragments of his *Lycurgeia* give us some idea what it would be like. In my discussion of one of these (above, pp. 42–3), I have pointed out that Aeschylus imitates a real primitive ritual while Euripides translates it into Greek lyric form. Perhaps one reason for this is the fact that Euripides is writing about Greek rather than foreign violence. The following discussion will show that, in spite of the atmosphere of wildness and strangeness, there is really very little about the forms of foreign religions in *Bacchae* or in any of the other plays of Euripides. Euripides' vivid and realistic description of the behavior of the bacchants emphasizes states of soul rather than details of foreign ritual.[25]

Of references to the Cretan rites only one (*Bacch.* 120–5) contains any real "lore." This describes the Curetes and Corybantes discovering the tympanum in

25. E. R. Dodds ("Maenadism in the *Bacchae*," *Harvard Theological Review*, 33 [1940], 155–76; and Euripides, *Bacchae*, ed. E. R. Dodds [2nd ed. Oxford, 1960], xi–l) has assembled evidence to show that maenadism is a psychological and historical fact which Euripides describes with clinical exactness.

the cave where Zeus was born. The same incident seems to be referred to earlier (*Bacch.* 55–61), with the implication that it took place in Phrygia rather than Crete. As we have seen, such indefiniteness is not unusual in Euripides' treatment of foreign material. A fragment (fr. 472 *Cretes*) contains another and more extensive reference to Cretan ritual. A chorus of initiates in the mysteries of Zeus-Zagreus describe their holy life as *βάκχοι* of the Curetes, who have performed the sacred rite of omophagy and carried torches for the mountain mother. There is no special information here. All these aspects of Cretan worship are familiar from *Bacchae* or the mountain mother choruses of *Hippolytus* and *Helen.* The reference at the end to pure white garments and a vegetarian diet seems to be peculiar to Cretan ritual. Like the choruses of *Bacchae* this fragment is romantically exotic rather than realistically foreign.[26] The references to the Cretan religion in *Hippolytus* say nothing concrete about ritual or belief. The chorus refer to the Corybantes and the mountain mother. They call Dictynna by Artemis' cult name, *πολύθηρος* (*Hipp.* 141–50). They name Dictynna once again (*Hipp.* 1130). In all these passages Dictynna is a counterpart of Artemis, a common

26. Kranz (*Stasimon*, p. 109) finds this passage so little in accord with his theory that Euripides' interest in foreign matters is late that he has to conclude, "Die Parodos der *Kreter* des Jahres 438 mit ihrer freilich sehr anschaulichen Schilderung des mystischen Kultes des idäisch Zeus wird kaum den Charakter des ganzen Stückes bestimmt haben." Kranz' theory is discussed in more detail below, n. 33.

identification in Greek cult. She is actually called Dictynna by Iphigenia's companions (*IT* 126–36).[27] Instead of emphasizing her foreign characteristics Euripides follows the practice of his day in assimilating her to a Greek goddess.

The Phrygian gods are also often mentioned. In *Troiades* there seems to be a description of an actual rite. The chorus speaks of all-night celebrations of the Trojans that took place every month, with choruses, *χρυσέων τε ξοάνων τύποι* (*Tro.* 1071–6). There is also an appeal in passing to *Κρόνιε, πρύτανι Φρύγιε* (*Tro.* 1288), but it tells us nothing further about Phrygian Zeus. The appeal of the Phrygian (*Or.* 1453) to the Idaian mother is of the same order, unless the epithet *ὄβριμα* has some special cult meaning we do not know about. The *ὄργια* of Cybele in *Bacchae* (78–80) are even less informative than the description from *Cretes*. In richness of foreign detail and outlandish sound effects they are not to be compared with the description of the revel from Aeschylus' *Edoni* (fr. 57). Except for the first, all these references to Phrygian divinities are cursory or formulaic.

The ode to the mountain mother at the crisis of *Helen* (1301–68) should perhaps have a special word. Its relation to the context is so unclear that some editors think it is interpolated either from another Euripidean play, or from a play by a different author. It is

27. See L. R. Farnell (*Cults of the Greek States* [5 vols. Oxford, 1896–1909], *2*, 476–7) for the identification of Artemis and Dictynna in Greece and Crete.

the only chorus of Euripides that Hofman will allow to be irrelevant.[28] But, whether or not it is by Euripides, its fits into the pattern I have been describing. Like the odes of *Bacchae* it has wildness and excitement but little specifically foreign content. The story of Demeter's search for Kore, and the blighting of nature, goes back to the Homeric hymn rather than to foreign ritual.[29] With characteristic vagueness the poet does not indicate whether the goddess of this ode belongs on Phrygian or Cretan Ida.[30]

28. Hans Herman Hofman (*Über den Zusammenhang zwischen Chorliedern und Handlung in den erhaltenen Dramen des Euripides* [diss. Leipzig, 1916], p. 106) regards this chorus as a true ἐμβόλιμον in the sense used by Aristotle (*Poetics* 1456a, 26–32). He thinks it belonged in some other play of Euripides and was inserted in the central place in *Helen* by some actor or director more interested in stage effects than continuity, and cites Heath, Hermann, and Decharme in support of this view. John G. Griffith ("Some Thoughts on 'Helena' of Euripides," *J.H.S.*, 73 [1953], 36, n. 14) promises to publish an article in which he will demonstrate that this ode has an aetiological connection with the story of Helen in Egypt. As far as I know this article has never appeared.

29. I have found no comment on the fact that the part of this ode that describes the rivers and the sea (*Helen* 1301–7) imitates the sound of the Dionysiac instruments in which Demeter finds comfort (*Helen* 1346–52), or vice versa. Does the poet intend to suggest an aetiology for the foreign musical instruments in the Dionysiac cult?

30. The ode is addressed to a woman suffering from an unnamed affliction which the chorus attributes to her failure properly to honor the great mother goddess. The situation would fit a Stheneboia or a Phaedra. In fact the chorus of *Hippolytus* (141 ff) makes the same supposition about

We learn few details about the rites of Taurian Artemis, although they are often referred to. We know only that they are bloody, secret, and revolting (*IT* 69–75, 224–8); that the victim must be ritually pure (*IT* 1157–1202, 1222–33); that Iphigenia is in charge of the preliminary ritual; and that the actual sacrifice is performed by someone else inside the temple (*IT* 34–41, 617–24), after which the victim is burned and thrown into a chasm (*IT* 625–6). Except for the fact that the victim is a human being, the ritual conforms to accepted Greek practice.[31]

In addition to the above, there are passing references to Ammon (*Alc.* 116; *El.* 734–5), in both cases more as a geographical designation than a god; to Thracian Dionysus (*Hec.* 1267); to Orpheus, if he may be considered a foreigner (*Cyc.* 646; *Hipp.* 952–4).

As a rule Euripides in characterizing barbarians disregards differences in manners and social institutions. His foreign characters behave like Greeks. Contrast, for example, his Hecuba with Aeschylus' Atossa—both Oriental queens, but how different in manners. On a few occasions, for some specific purpose, he shows detailed information about foreign institutions and man-

Phaedra's mysterious illness. If the ode really belongs to one of Euripides' lost plays I suggest it might have been *Stheneboia* or *Hippolytus Veiled*. If the first the goddess referred to would be Phrygian, if the second Cretan.

31. See, for instance, the description of the ritual at Delphi in H. W. Parke and D. E. W. Wormell, *The Delphic Oracle* (2 vols. Oxford, 1956), *1*, 27–34.

ners; but he does not sustain and elaborate it through a whole play as Aeschylus does.

Two passages in *Andromache* show that Euripides knew something about the marriage customs of Thrace and Phrygia. Andromache is advising Hermione on how to deal with an unfaithful husband (*Andr.* 215–18).

> εἰ δ᾽ ἀμφὶ Θρῄκην χιόνι τὴν κατάρρυτον
> τύραννον ἔσχες ἄνδρ᾽, ἵν᾽ ἐν μέρει λέχος
> δίδωσι πολλαῖς εἷς ἀνὴρ κοινούμενος,
> ἔκτεινας ἂν τάσδ᾽;

Euripides could have gotten this information from Herodotus (5.16). Wherever he got it, it is not one of these bits of stock characterization, like his occasional references to foreign servility and effeminacy. Andromache continues (*Andr.* 222–8),

> ὦ φίλταθ᾽ Ἕκτορ, ἀλλ᾽ ἐγὼ τὴν σὴν χάριν
> σοι καὶ ξυνήρων, εἴ τί σε σφάλλοι Κύπρις,
> καὶ μαστὸν ἤδη πολλάκις νόθοισι σοῖς
> ἐπέσχον, ἵνα σοι μηδὲν ἐνδοίην πικρόν.
> καὶ ταῦτα δρῶσα τῇ ἀρετῇ προσηγόμην
> πόσιν. σὺ δ᾽ οὐδὲ ῥανίδ᾽ ὑπαιθρίας δρόσου
> τῷ σῷ προσίζειν ἀνδρὶ δειμαίνουσ᾽ ἐᾷς.

Homer could have been the source for the facts in this passage, but not for the act of imagination with which Euripides finds his way to the human content of an alien custom. Hermione's vulgar conclusion that all barbarians are "immoral" would be the reaction of the unimaginative Greek "common man" to a foreign institution he did not understand. However, the difference between Greek and barbarian manners indicated in this passage is not something emphasized or developed throughout the play. The subject is introduced, not to show how foreign Andromache is, but to show how civilized and womanly she is in comparison with the supposedly civilized Hermione.

In the scene with the Phrygian in *Orestes*, Euripides represents foreign customs and behavior with uncharacteristic vividness and detail. But the foreign references here, like those in *Andromache*, are not sustained and developed throughout the play. The Phrygian has his one scene—a genre piece, which reminds us on the one hand of Aeschylus' outlandish barbarian effects, on the other of the unsympathetic realism of Timotheus' *Persae*—and appears no more. The scene stands out because it has nothing in common with the tone of the rest of the play.

In this scene Euripides shows quite specific information about the Persian or Phrygian practice of using eunuchs as boudoir servants (see above, p. 80). Orestes and Pylades discuss the custom with contempt (*Or.* 1110–14).

> Ορ. καὶ πῶς; ἔχει γὰρ βαρβάρους ὀπάονας.
> Πυ. τίνας; Φρυγῶν γὰρ οὐδέν᾽ ἂν τρέσαιμ᾽ ἐγώ.
> Ορ. οἵους ἐνόπτρων καὶ μύρων ἐπιστάτας.
> Πυ. τρυφὰς γὰρ ἥκει δεῦρ᾽ ἔχουσα Τρωικάς;
> Ορ. ὥσθ᾽ Ἑλλὰς αὐτῇ σμικρὸν οἰκητήριον.

There is a real touch of the harem in the scene described by the Phrygian (*Or.* 1426–30),

> Φρυγίοις ἔτυχον Φρυγίοισι νόμοις
> παρὰ βόστρυχον αὔραν αὔραν
> Ἑλένας Ἑλένας εὐπαγεῖ
> κύκλῳ πτερίνῳ πρὸ παρηίδος
> ἀίσσων βαρβάροις νόμοισιν.

Contrast the exotic atmosphere of this scene with the Trojan boudoir scene in *Hecuba* (see above, pp. 125–6). The *Hecuba* scene, as I have already suggested, is essentially the boudoir scene of Greek vase painting. The *Orestes* scene, with the barbarian music and the eunuch waving the circular feathered fan, is one of the rare scenes in Euripides which really gets outside the Greek context.

Like Aeschylus' Persians, the Phrygian greets Orestes with a salaam (*Or.* 1507),

> προσκυνῶ σ', ἄναξ, νόμοισι βαρβάροισι προσπίτνων,

at which Orestes, shocked, says,

> οὐκ ἐν Ἰλίῳ τάδ' ἐστίν, ἀλλ' ἐν Ἀργείᾳ χθονί.

This custom is also mentioned in *Troiades* (1020–1), again in connection with Helen's servants, when Hecuba accuses Helen of wanting Trojan adulation.

> ἐν τοῖς Ἀλεξάνδρου γὰρ ὕβριζες δόμοις
> καὶ προσκυνεῖσθαι βαρβάρων ὕπ' ἤθελες.
> μεγάλα γὰρ ἦν σοι.

It is also the style of greeting natural to the Phoenician women when they meet Polyneices (*Phoen.* 293–4).

> γονυπετεῖς ἕδρας προσπίτνω σ', ἄναξ,
> τὸν οἴκοθεν νόμον σέβουσ'.

This is the *only* reference Euripides makes to the native customs of the chorus of this play. He achieves his effect of strangeness, not with specific detail about dress, appearance, speech, and behavior, as Aeschylus does in *Suppliants*, but by representing the chorus as incoherent and excitable, and by constant use of the word βάρβαρος or its equivalent Φοίνισσα (see above, pp. 116–20).

One other reference to Phrygian manners may be seen in *Troiades* (1209–13). When Hecuba is wrapping the body of Astyanax in Hector's robes she says,

> ὦ τέκνον, οὐχ ἵπποισι νικήσαντά σε
> οὐδ' ἥλικας τόξοισιν, οὓς Φρύγες νόμους
> τιμῶσιν, οὐκ ἐς πλησμονὰς θηρωμένη,
> μήτηρ πατρός σοι προστίθησ' ἀγάλματα
> τῶν σῶν ποτ' ὄντων.

This is the stock picture of the young Phrygian with his bow and his horse. Like Sophocles' fragment 775 (see above, p. 82) it might have been inspired by Herodotus' description of Persian education. But facts like these are not part of the characterizations of the play. If all such references were cut out the play would have lost nothing essential.

As compared with Aeschylus, Euripides shows very

little interest in Egyptian custom or belief. The ritual of Theonoe's entrance is perhaps meant to give an effect of barbarous splendor (*Helen* 865–72), and the purification of the air with a torch is a known piece of Egyptian ritual, the only one in the play, so far as I can discover.[32] Theonoe's belief in punishment for sins after death is as Pindaric as it is Egyptian (*Helen* 1013–16), and Theoclymenus' discounting of the after life (*Helen* 1421) seems to contradict Egyptian belief as reported by Herodotus (2.123). So does his respect for foreign custom (*Helen* 1241–4; cf. Hdt. 2.79, 91, and above, p. 35). His hostility to Greeks is attributed not to xenophobia but to jealousy over Helen (*Helen* 468–83). None of the Egyptians shows any trace of foreign manners. Like Shakespeare's Bohemians they are a conveniently remote people without any recognizable national characteristics. One difference in religious usage is pointed out. Helen says that Proteus' tomb affords her sanctuary, just as a temple or altar would in Greece (*Helen* 800–1).

Like the Egyptians the Taurian natives lack specific national characteristics. In the two long messenger scenes (*IT* 238–391, 1284–1419), which describe them fairly minutely, they appear more as primitives than

32. It was first observed by Samuel Musgrave (*Euripidis tragoediae, fragmenta, epistolae* [3 vols. Leipzig, 1788], *3*, ad loc.) that the ritual of purifying the air with a torch for the priestess is ascribed to the Egyptian priests by Plutarch (*Moralia* 383b, *de Iside et Osiride*, 4). Musgrave concludes "Hinc patet, Euripidem in egressu Theionoës depingendo ab historiae fide non discessisse."

as foreigners. In their simplicity they first take the strangers for gods, then, lacking other weapons, attack them with stones. They summon help by blowing on κόχλοι, great shells of a kind that are often excavated in Greece today—the standard noisemaking instrument of ancient shepherds and other poor folk. Nothing distinguishes them from Greek shepherds, and no foreign manners have been given to Thoas.

The Cyclops is also a primitive—the sophist's idea of man without law. His manners belong to no culture. He is not a Sicel but a child of nature, and does not properly belong in this discussion. I find no sign that Euripides ever tries to equate barbarian and primitive. His one discussion of man's evolution from primitivism (*Supp.* 195–218) certainly does not suggest it. When Theseus describes how some god, by the gift of intelligence, speech, and the arts, helped men escape from a squalid and bestial way of life, he makes no distinction between Greek and barbarian, but speaks of all mankind.

Nine passages in the fragments refer to foreign customs or manners. He mentions the gardens of Adonis (fr. 514 *Melanippe*), the wealth of Merops (fr. 781 *Phaethon*). Three fragments refer to Thracians. The Thracian invaders of Eleusis are an uncouth lot (fr. 367 *Erechtheus*),

ἐν ἀστρώτῳ πέδῳ
εὕδουσι, πηγαῖς δ' οὐχ ὑγραίνουσιν πόδας.

Paxithea indicates that the Thracians are very different from the Athenians, but adds no concrete details (fr. 360 *Erechtheus*). The passage is corrupt (lines 46–9), but she clearly implies that the presence of the Thracians in Athens would be some kind of profanation. Apparently the exotic music of the Thracians was mentioned (fr. 370 *Erechtheus*). The remaining four passages (fr. 139 *Andromeda;* fr. 719 *Telephus;* fr. 796 *Philoctetes;* fr. 907 inc.) bring up the problem of inferiority and superiority.

In Euripides by far the largest class of references to foreign institutions and manners has to do with the conflict of Greek and barbarian, with supposed barbarian inferiority and its converse Greek superiority.[33]

33. Kranz (*Stasimon*, pp. 109–12) correctly observes that Euripides gives the problem of the relative merits of Greek and barbarian much greater prominence than do Aeschylus and Sophocles. He tries to show that there is a gradually increasing emphasis on barbarian problems from the early to the late plays, and attributes this to Euripides' return to the manner of Aeschylus in his later work. We lack evidence of such a development. What Kranz takes for evidence are two rather common misconceptions, (1) that *Medea* and plays of that period make less of the foreign element than *Bacchae* and plays of that period, (2) that Euripides' treatment of foreigners like the followers of Dionysus and the Phoenician women is the result of imitating Aeschylus. The first assumption overlooks the fact that one of the important themes of *Medea* is foreignness, though the externals of foreignness are not emphasized in that play. The second assumption overlooks the fact (discussed above, pp. 140 ff) that the foreign local color of *Bacchae* is indefinite and vague, while the local

The idea that Greeks are natural rulers of barbarians occurs twice in *Andromache* (647–54, 662–7), three times in *Iphigenia in Aulis* (952–4, 1264–75, 1400–1). The superiority of the Greek rule of law to the barbarian concept of tyranny is mentioned in *Medea* (532–41), *Heracleidae* (423–4), and *Helen* (276). The moral inferiority of barbarians is a favorite theme. It occurs in *Medea* (591–2, 1330–43), *Andromache* (173–6, 243, 261–2, 870), *Hecuba* (328–31, 877, 1129), *Orestes* (485, 1110–15, 1508, 1527–8), *Bacchae* (481–3), *Iphigenia in Aulis* (270–2). Once we find the concept of an inevitable natural hostility of Greek and barbarian (*Hec.* 1199–1201), and occasionally the barbarians take their turn at looking down on the Greeks (*Tro.* 764, 1190–1; *IT* 1174). In none of these passages are there any facts about particular nationalities. They are simply assertions about the genus non-Greek. Other indications of this emphasis on conflict are Euripides' formulaic reiteration of the word *βάρβαρος*, and the special pejorative sense he has

---

color in foreign plays of Aeschylus is definite and concrete. We are not in a position to say what Euripides' attitude may have been in his early plays. His earliest extant play, *Alcestis*, is already late. We have seen (above, n. 26) that its companion piece *Cretes* contains too much foreign material to suit Kranz's theory. The theme of foreignness is as pervasive in *Medea*, *Andromache*, and *Hecuba* as it is in *Bacchae*, more so than it is in *Phoenissae* and *Orestes*. The method of presenting the theme is indeed very different in different plays, but the theme itself was not a late acquired interest, but an important preoccupation throughout the period for which we have evidence.

for it (see above, pp. 12–13). The content of this class of references and their relation to Euripides' own ideas about foreigners are beyond the scope of this study. For my present purpose it is sufficient to point out that they are much more frequent and complex in Euripides than they are in either Aeschylus or Sophocles.

In representing foreign religion and manners Euripides is characteristically vague. He refers to foreign religion rather often because he could hardly write *Bacchae* and *Hippolytus* and the Trojan plays without doing so. We should not forget that *Helen* and *Iphigenia Among the Taurians* practically ignore the question. If the plays of Aeschylus involving the cults of Dionysus, Triptolemus, Cybele, and other foreign gods had survived, what quantities of lore and ritual we should expect to find in them! Judged by this standard the information we find in Euripides about Cretan, Lydian, and Phrygian gods is thin. On foreign customs in general Euripides occasionally shows himself informed, but he does not create and sustain for a whole play a specific national type of behavior, as Aeschylus does in *Suppliants* and *Persae*. The Phrygian of *Orestes* is the only carefully created foreign type in the extant plays of Euripides, and he is only an incidental character. His bizarre behavior, coming just at the climax of the action, has somewhat the effect of Osric in Hamlet—an unforeseen note of comedy at a moment of great tension. And the Phrygian is unique. In *Helen*, *Iphigenia Among the*

Taurians, and the Trojan plays, Euripides passes up the opportunity to create such types. Of the three writers he apparently bothers least about foreign customs and manners, in spite of the fact that he has such a large number of important foreign characters in his plays.

When Euripides does distinguish Trojans from Greeks he follows Sophocles in giving them Persian national traits—witness the Phrygian eunuch, Andromache's views on marriage, Hecuba's reference to the pastimes of Persian youths. Perhaps the word παρασάγγης in *Scyrii* (fr. 686) occurred in such a context. But such suggestions are rare and incidental. Polyxena and Andromache are not noticeably foreigners as Aeschylus' Cassandra is, or, as I have suggested, the Trojans of Sophocles' lost plays may have been.

Euripides is further distinguished from Aeschylus and Sophocles by his interest in the question of the relative value of Greek and barbarian culture and individuals. This subject is occasionally raised by Aeschylus and dealt with at some length by Sophocles in *Ajax* and *Tereus*, but with Euripides it is a major preoccupation. I have listed twenty-six such passages in the plays (above, p. 152), ranging from passing comments to major debates. This is certainly not all. Of the nine fragments dealing with foreign behavior, four raise the question of inferiority. This is a shift in interest. For Euripides, in contrast to Aeschylus and Sophocles, manners, beliefs, behavior, of given nationalities are of secondary importance. What matters is not *how* a character is foreign, but *that* he is foreign. References to foreign traits are sketchy and incidental. References to *the fact* of being a foreigner, and therefore an inferior, are frequent. They remind us of something we might otherwise forget—that the person before us on the stage, though he talks and acts like a Greek, is in fact a stranger and an outsider.

Geography

Of the three dramatists Euripides has the largest number of geographical references. These contain, in proportion to their numbers, very little information. Although there are almost three times as many extant plays of Euripides as there are of either Sophocles or Aeschylus, and many more fragments, Euripides uses only a few more place names than Sophocles (77 as compared with 61), and a good many less than Aeschylus (100, see Appendix). In contrast to his two predecessors his approach is formulaic and tends to repetition—hence the relatively small number of names. I have indicated occasional formulaic use of geographic names by Aeschylus and Sophocles (above, pp. 31–2, 45, 76, 94). But in Aeschylus, and probably also in Sophocles, there is also a lively treatment of geographical fact. In Euripides we find much less of this, while the number of what I call stock references is high.[34]

34. Wilamowitz in a passage already referred to (n. 9, p. 73 and n. 44, p. 101) briefly discusses Euripides' lack of interest in facts about foreign peoples and particularly in foreign

I have already mentioned some of the more familiar formulae (above, p. 127)—the Tyrrhenian trumpets; the Asiatic, Libyan, and Phrygian musical instruments; and the Thracian shields—all of which occur fairly frequently in the plays. The many references to Trojan wealth and luxury might also be called formulaic. In the same category are the waterless sons of Ammon (meaning Libya, *Alc.* 115–16; *El.* 734–5); Chalybian iron (*Alc.* 980); Thrace, in connection with bad weather (*Cyc.* 329; *Alc.* 67; *Andr.* 215; *Hec.* 81); Thrace, in connection with horses (*Hec.* 7–9, 428, 710, 1090); Enetian colts (*Hipp.* 231, 1131); various ways of referring to the ends of the earth, Pontus and Atlantic (*Hipp.* 3, 1053); Nile and Phasis (*Andr.* 650–1); Ocean (*Or.* 1377); *Φρυγῶν πόλις, γαῖα,* or *χθών*, as a synonym for Troy (*Cyc.* 284; *Andr.* 194, 291, 363, 455; *Hec.* 4, 1141; *Tro.* 7, 994; *IA* 773, 1197, 1290, 1525). Notice how often the same, or a similar phrase, is reused. In the extant plays the smaller number of names of foreign peoples and places, and the much higher proportion of repetitions, is also an indication of his more formulaic approach. For example, in *Suppliants* Aeschylus uses 23 names 36 times; Euripides in his Egyptian play, *Helen*, uses 16 names 64 times (see Appendix).

Symplegades are referred to (not always by name) in thirteen places (*Medea* 2, 432, 1263; *Andr.* 794, 864; *IT* 124–5, 241, 260, 355, 392–5, 746, 889–90,

---

geography, and contrasts it with the attitude of Sophocles. This difference generally goes unobserved.

1389), but none of the references visualizes and localizes an actual place as Aeschylus does even in his glancing references (e.g., the description of the Bosporus region quoted pp. 55–6 above). Euripides' purpose is not description. For him the foreign place name is an evocative word, suggesting distance, danger, and an inhospitable land.

ὦ
κυανεᾶν λιποῦσα Συμπληγάδων
πετρᾶν ἀξενωτάταν ἐσβολάν . . .
(*Medea* 1263–4)

. . . διὰ κυανέας μὴν
στενοπόρου πέτρας μακρὰ κέλευθα . . .
(*IT* 889–90)

I have picked the most concrete and circumstantial examples I could find. Six out of twelve times Symplegades occurs in combination with some form of ἄξεινος, or other way of referring to the Black Sea (*Andr.* 793–4; *IT* 124–5, 392–5, 1388; *Medea* 432–3, 1263–4). This amounts to a formula—a poetic way of naming the Black Sea. Variations of this formula run through *Iphigenia Among the Taurians* like a refrain, accentuating the theme of loneliness and homesickness.

The other references to the ἄξεινος πόντος (it is εὔξεινος only once, in Thetis' happy prophecy about Achilles, *Andr.* 1262) are equally vague (*HF* 410–11; *IT* 94, 218, 253, 341, 438). The phrase Μαιῶτιν ἄμφι πολυπόταμον (*HF* 409–10) does show that he knows one of the principal characteristics of the region, and in another passage (*IT* 421–38) he names Symplegades, Salmydessus, and Leuke Akte in geographical order. But in the same place he manages to convey the idea that Leuke Akte, near the mouth of the Danube, is Orestes' destination. Elsewhere he suggests that the Taurians live *on* or *by* the Symplegades (*IT* 124–5),

> πόντου δισσὰς συγχωρούσας
> πέτρας Ἀξείνου ναίοντες.

He also seems to imply that the land of the Taurians is in Asia (*IT* 392–7, also perhaps 180)—something Aeschylus and Herodotus, and probably Sophocles, would deny (see above, pp. 50–3, 98). But I think it is a mistake to press these passages for geographical information.

It is probably not ignorance that makes Euripides vague and inaccurate. The fact is that for his particular poetic purpose it does not matter whether he is geographically accurate or not. To give the idea that Leuke Akte and the land of the Taurians are side by side makes no more difference than Shakespeare's giving Bohemia a sea coast. What matters is the feeling of distance and danger evoked by the names, not their actual location. Unlike Sophocles and Aeschylus, Euripides does not use geographical references to localize his story and make it real, but to create an atmosphere, in this case of strangeness and abandonment—rather to make it unreal. Most of the references I have been discussing come from *Iphigenia Among the*

Taurians where strangeness and abandonment are important themes. In this play of course there is an obvious practical reason for referring to the Black Sea region, but the refrainlike frequency and formulaic quality of the references suggests that Euripides is using them thematically to produce an effect of loneliness and abandonment in a hostile land. For this purpose accurate detail is irrelevant.

There are flashes of geographical information in Euripides that prove he is not ignorant. He has no large-scale geographical passages, but he has some fairly circumstantial brief ones. He makes two positive statements about the causes of the Nile flood (*Helen* 2–3; fr. 228 *Archelaus*).

> [Nile] ὃς ἀντὶ δίας ψακάδος Αἰγύπτου πέδον
> λευκῆς τακείσης χιόνος ὑγραίνει γύας.

> Δαναὸς ὁ πεντήκοντα θυγατέρων πατὴρ
> Νείλου λιπὼν κάλλιστον ἐκ γαίας ὕδωρ,
> ὃς ἐκ μελαμβρότοιο πληροῦται ῥοὰς
> Αἰθιοπίδος γῆς, ἡνίκ᾽ ἂν τακῇ χιὼν
> τέθριππ᾽ ἄγοντος ἡλίου κατ᾽ αἰθέρα,
> ἐλθὼν ἐς Ἄργος ᾤκισ᾽ Ἰνάχου πόλιν.

The parallel fragment of Aeschylus (fr. 300 inc. quoted above, p. 55) has a reality that Euripides does not even attempt. Aeschylus has material details —the seven-mouthed Nile rolling earth, the rocklike snow, Demeter's sheaves. Euripides' description is vague and generalized. And yet we know that he too could make scenes when he wished—for example, in the descriptions of *Bacchae.*

He knows that Egypt and Libya are rainless (*Alc.* 115–16; *El.* 734–5, see above, p. 156; and probably *Helen* 1485 and *Bacch.* 406–8), that the coast of Libya is harborless (*Helen* 404, 1211), but these are passing references, unembellished by detail. This is all that Euripides has to say about Egypt and Libya. He seems to have gotten the idea for the plot of *Helen* from Herodotus, and dispensed with almost all of Herodotus' information about Egypt.[35]

Perhaps the most specific piece of foreign geo-

35. For possible influence of Herodotus on Euripides see W. Nestle, "Untersuchungen über die philosophischen Quellen des Euripides," *Philologus,* suppl. 8 (1901), 652–4, and Joseph Wells, *Studies in Herodotus* (Oxford, 1923), p. 187. A good many parallels exist. Nestle regards them as proofs of influence. Wells thinks all but the story of Helen in Egypt (*Helen* and *El.* 1280–3) are accidental. But even here the historian and the tragedian have different versions. Neither Nestle nor Wells mentions the fact that Herodotus (4.103) says the Taurians sacrifice Greek strangers to a maiden goddess whom they call Iphigeneia, daughter of Agamemnon. The question can hardly be settled, since all the coincidences are in the realm of concept rather than fact, e.g., Solon's maxim (Hdt. 1.29 ff, and *Andr.* 100–02; *Heracl.* 863–6; *Tro. 509–10*), and the criticism of tyranny (Hdt. 5.92, and *Supp. 447–55*). Common traditions and common reactions to intellectual and historical events of the 5th century seem to me a sufficient explanation for this type of parallel. But whatever plots and ideas Euripides may have taken from Herodotus, it is clear that he left the great store of information about Phrygia, Persia, Colchis, the Taurians, Egypt, Ethiopia almost untouched.

graphical information we have from Euripides is in *Bacchae* (462–3).

> Δι. τὸν ἀνθεμώδη Τμῶλον οἶσθά που κλύων.
> Πε. οἶδ', ὃς τὸ Σαρδέων ἄστυ περιβάλλει κύκλῳ.

The excavator of Sardis thinks the description applies to the site, which suggests that Euripides really knew something about the situation of Sardis.[36] Elsewhere he speaks of Tmolus as running with gold (*Bacch.* 154), another piece of genuine information (see Hdt. 1.93). When he speaks of Aetna as opposite the Phoenician land (*Tro.* 220–2) he again shows some sense of geographical location, but no special research was needed for the epithet "firedripping" which is applied to it in *Cyclops* (298).

It seems possible that the myth that the sun changed its course in horror at the crimes of Atreus and Thyestes (*El.* 726–36; *Or.* 1001–7; *IT* 193, 817) may reflect Herodotus' version of the tradition of the Sothic year in Egypt (2.142). But it is doubtful if Euripides thought of this even if it is true.

There are other odds and ends of information. According to Pliny (*Naturalis Historia* 37.31, quoted in *TGF*, p. 24) he made the Rhodanus and the Padus flow together into the Adriatic. Does this make him

36. H. C. Butler in *Sardis; Publications of the American Society for the Excavation of Sardis* (Leyden n.d.), *1*, Part II, 21. "Euripides describes the earlier city as encircled by Mt. Tmolos, which would suggest that the original site was entirely within the space between the Akropolis and Nekropolis Hills, extending well up the valley and its slopes."

better informed than Aeschylus who, according to the same authority, identified Eridanus and Rhodanus as one river which he located in Spain? Euripides derives the name Phoenicia (Phoinikia) from Phoinix, Cilicia (Kilikia) from Kilix, sons of Agenor (fr. 819 *Phrixus*), just as he derives Ionia from Ion in the play of that name (1581–8). Occasionally he indulges his imagination in some fabulous geography—the mythical western lands, Atlas, the gardens of the Hesperides, Eridanus, and the amber tears that the daughters of Helius dropped into the Padus (*Hipp.* 735–51 and the passage of Pliny referred to above), the wanderings of Odysseus (*Tro.* 433–41), the foreign labors of Heracles (*HF* 375–424), the land of the rising sun and the palace of the sun (fr. 771, 773 *Phaethon*).

More characteristic of Euripides' use of geographical material are some passages which might, because of their vividness, be called geographical, but which essentially are not. He describes very beautifully the cranes that winter in Libya (*Helen* 1479–89).

δι' ἀέρος εἴθε ποτανοὶ
γενοίμεσθ' ᾇ Λιβύας
οἰωνοὶ στοχάδες
ὄμβρον λιποῦσαι χειμέριον
νίσονται πρεσβυτάτᾳ
σύριγγι πείθομεναι
ποιμένος, ὃς ἄβροχα πεδία καρποφόρα τε γᾶς
ἐπιπετόμενος ἰαχεῖ.
Ὦ πταναὶ δολιαύχενες,

σύννομοι νεφέων δρόμου,
βᾶτε.

There is great vividness in the longnecked cloud dwellers following their leader's piping from the stormy north to the fertile rainless fields (of Egypt, one presumes). But the setting is subordinated to the mood of freedom and escape the poet conveys through the picture of the great birds disporting themselves in the clouds. The birds dominate the scene. The landscape is vague.

The reflecting of the sunrise on Mt. Ida, vivid as it is, could apply to the eastern face of any mountain, and does not indicate special knowledge of the Troad (*Tro.* 1066–70).

Ἰδαῖά τ' Ἰδαῖα κισσοφόρα νάπη
χιόνι κατάρυτα ποταμίᾳ
τέρμονα πρωτόβολον θ' ἁλίῳ,
τὰν καταλαμπομέναν ζαθέαν θεράπναν.

When Euripides describes the journey of the Phoenissae from Tyre to Thebes (*Phoen.* 202–14), while he shows that he knows about the island of Tyre, he gives an improbable route. If the maidens were going to Thebes why did they not land at a port on the Gulf of Salamis, or at Aulis, instead of going all around Peloponnesus and through the Corinthian Gulf? This might make sense if they were going straight to Delphi. Cirrha (modern Itea) to Delphi is a short trip, but Thebes is approached with difficulty from the Corinthian Gulf. I suggest Euripides did not bother about this detail. He liked the traditional route—the route of Apollo from Delos to Delphi—and did not stop to remember that his chorus was not going direct to Delphi. Again, geography is not the point.[37]

The journey of Dionysus and his followers (*Bacch.* 13–22) gives the appearance rather than the reality of a geographical passage. Πολύχρυσος is a stock epithet for Lydia and Phrygia, but the clear distinction between the sunstruck plains of Persia, harsh Media, and Araby "the blest," prepare us for a real description which never comes. In spite of Strabo's criticism (see above, p. 96) it is not impossible to reconstruct the journey from the list of places on Dionysus' route. He starts in Lydia and travels east through Phrygia to Persia, then north to Bactria, and back through Media and Arabia to Asia Minor, thus making the circuit of Asia. But Euripides is not interested in Dionysus' route as Aeschylus is interested in Io's or Sophocles in Triptolemus' (see above, pp. 96–7). By proper use of names and epithets he has given an impression of the distant and the exotic. The itinerary is secondary.

Euripides, as we saw, disregards differences of dress,

37. Kranz (*Stasimon*, p. 110) eliminates this difficulty by assuming that the chorus went first to Delphi, then to Thebes. This is unlikely since lines 222 ff imply that they had not yet performed the ritual that precedes admission to the temple. ἔτι δὲ Κασταλίας ὕδωρ περιμένει με . . . See Ion's instructions to the chorus (*Ion* 95–7) and Miller's comments on the two passages (*Daedalus and Thespis*, *1*, 48).

language, and behavior and often represents foreigners as though they were Greeks. Occasionally, as with the Phrygian of *Orestes*, or Andromache's defense of concubinage, he throws in some authentic local color, but he never makes it a fundamental part of his work. He handles foreign geography in the same way. For the most part he neglects the opportunity for foreign effects afforded by the settings of *Helen*, *Iphigenia Among the Taurians*, *Troiades*, *Hecuba*, and, as far as we can tell, *Phaethon* and *Andromeda*. In *Helen*, *Troiades*, and *Hecuba* setting is almost entirely ignored. When he does describe foreign landscape he does not attempt foreign effects. The rocky caves and coast of *Iphigenia Among the Taurians* have nothing specifically foreign about them—nothing that distinguishes them, for instance, from the lonely shores of Lemnos in *Philoctetes*. There are no specifically Sicilian elements in the rude pastoral landscape of *Cyclops*. The morning song of *Phaethon* (fr. 773) describes a beautiful and romantic scene in the land of the rising sun, but it is an idyllic not a foreign scene —not so much fabulous geography as Aeschylus would have treated it, well mapped out and peopled with gods, demigods, and monsters by the mythmaking imagination, as a pastoral scene with a touch of otherworldliness, a spiritual landscape. As far as we can judge, *Andromeda* also belonged in this category of foreign plays in which the setting is dissolved in a misty romanticism that takes little account of traditional lore or ascertainable fact about the people and places concerned.[38]

If Euripides treated foreign places concretely and specifically in any of the lost plays, it should show in the fragments. It is the quaint fact and the rare place name that get quoted by essayists and lexicographers, as we saw in the case of Sophocles. Of the three dramatists Euripides has the largest number of fragments containing the smallest number of geographical references. The distribution of place names between extant plays and fragments gives us a rough idea of the differences between the three writers in this respect. The fragments of Euripides contain less than a third of the total number of foreign names that he uses, those of Aeschylus a good deal more than a third, and those of Sophocles more than three quarters. About a tenth of the total number of names used by Euripides occur *only* in the fragments; about a fifth of the names used by Aeschylus and more than half of the names used by Sophocles occur *only* in their fragments (see Appendix). The reason why there is so little foreign material in the fragments of Euripides is, I think, that his repetitive, formulaic, uninformative, geographical references (in contrast to those of Aeschylus and Sophocles) are not quotable. They contain neither

38. Perhaps we have here an early predecessor of the "spiritual landscape" of Vergilian eclogue, which is described by Bruno Snell (*The Discovery of the Mind*, trans. by T. G. Rosenmeyer [Oxford, 1953], Ch. 13, "Arcadia: the Discovery of a Spiritual Landscape," pp. 281 ff).

little known facts, nor strange words, and so have not been preserved. The difference between the figures of Aeschylus and Sophocles is probably due, as I have already suggested (above, p. 112), to the accidents of survival.

Foreign geography in Euripides shows the same tendencies as other types of foreign references. Though he has a very large number of references, Euripides is thinnest in content, repeats most, and uses least concrete information. As elsewhere he generalizes foreignness into a single vaguely exotic concept, instead of breaking it down, as Aeschylus and Sophocles do, into groups of concrete characteristics and facts attached to specific peoples and places. He is occasionally well informed, but on the whole careless of geographical detail because it is not essential to his poetic purpose. He seldom wishes to present a particular place or people. He uses it often formulaically, always subordinately, for the creation of atmosphere and mood.

Conclusion

Aeschylus, Sophocles, and Euripides have roughly the same proportion of plays involving foreigners. Though Sophocles uses more Trojan stories than Aeschylus and Euripides, the important differences in their use of foreign material for dramatic purposes are not in subject matter but in treatment. In this respect Aeschylus and Sophocles are far more alike than is usually thought. Euripides is in a class by himself. Both

Aeschylus and Sophocles use detailed information about the different types of foreigners they represent. The fact that their information is not always accurate is not as important as the fact that they thought accuracy was necessary. Perhaps most of the inaccuracies are unintentional, though a few—the representation of Trojans as Persians for instance—must have been conscious. In lyric and dialogue, foreign language and behavior are a consistent part of the characterization of non-Greeks. As a theme, however, foreignness, the idea of what it means to be foreign, scarcely occurs in Aeschylus and is rare in Sophocles. The presence of foreign material in the plays of Aeschylus is not a sign of archaism or orientalizing. In Sophocles it is not a sign of imitating the older poet. Their intention seems to have been realistic. That is, they tried to make their foreign characters and scenes like real foreign characters and scenes, and did not introduce them gratuitously for dramatic or decorative effect.

With Euripides the actual concrete foreigner—Ethiopian, Persian, Egyptian—disappears, and we have instead the symbolic foreigner. This does not mean that the foreigners of Aeschylus and Sophocles may not have been used symbolically too. But, whatever symbolic uses they may have had, they were first of all realistically presented. Euripides is interested only in the symbolic aspects of foreignness, and can therefore dispense with most of the concrete details the other two dramatists use. With him the theme of foreignness is everywhere, but technical details about foreign looks, customs, clothing, language are rare. Specific details indicating nationality such as we find in Aeschylus' *Suppliants* and *Persae*, and have evidence for in some of Sophocles' lost plays, are lacking. Foreign words occur only as atmosphere in lyric passages, never as characterization in dialogue. His foreign characters are distinguished from Greeks not by factual detail, but by a few formulae frequently repeated, and by the word *βάρβαρος* recurring as a persistent theme throughout many of the plays. He rarely differentiates between types of foreigners. National differences are unimportant, but the fact of foreignness, the problems it creates, and the mood of romance and unreality it can be used to evoke, are never to be forgotten. Where Aeschylus and Sophocles are realistic, Euripides is thematic and symbolic. As we have seen, this is a matter of poetic intent, not ignorance.

All three writers, then, strongly emphasize the foreignness of non-Greek characters—Aeschylus and Sophocles realistically, Euripides formulaically. One would expect, especially in those days of writer-composer-directors, that the staging would also emphasize foreignness. Each play would have its own décor suggesting Greekness or foreignness of characters and setting to the same degree the text did. This is one more small point in favor of the view that the early productions of Greek tragedy were not the elaborately and ornately formalized and standardized affairs we read about in the handbooks (see above, p. 28 with n. 13). To a later period the forms of tragedy must have seemed almost as alien as Xerxes seemed to a fifth century audience. The remote world of myth and choral song would call for an alien splendor and formalism in costuming and staging.

The question of foreign material in tragedy is part of the larger literary question of the mythological plot. The treatment of foreigners by each writer seems to me to be largely a function of the way he presents the world of myth, which is the world of Greek tragedy. Aeschylus and Sophocles present this world as in some sense real, located in a real past, the world of their own ancestors, whose deeds and sufferings and encounters with foreign people are the background for and the explanation of the present. Aeschylus, with his tremendously concrete sense of location in time as well as space (his genealogies are as specific as his journeys), his treatment of Phineus, Xerxes, and Glaucus, in one trilogy on one plain of reality, conveys the strongest sense that myth is history. His foreigners belong in a fully imagined world of many nations that extends in space from Colchis to the Pillars of Heracles, in time from Io to the present. Sophocles is not given to the large and orderly schemes which make possible the visualization of a whole world. And more than Aeschylus he presents contemporary situations through mythological events. But he keeps the world of those events intact and separated from the present. The political debates of *Oedipus Tyrannus* and *Antigone* are universal rather than modern, and their setting is not contemporary

Thebes, but Thebes a generation before the Trojan war. I expect that the foreigners of the lost plays from which so much specific foreign information comes were as richly embedded in their own reality as the guard of *Antigone*, or the herdsman of *Oedipus*.

Euripides, on the other hand, is antimythological, in the sense that he is committed to destroying the illusion that the events of myth ever took place in any literal sense. There is a powerful attack on the idea that myth is historical. His characters are contemporary, and they live in a contemporary world, where scientific or rationalistic explanations often supersede mythological ones. Heracles doubts he is the son of Zeus. Ion cannot believe Apollo fathered a bastard and abandoned him. The prehistoric maidens of *Ion* describe a temple at Delphi that was built by the Alcmaeonids. The prologue, the debate, the epiphany of the god, are often so artificially and woodenly handled that no one could imagine that they literally happened. In the same way we do not imagine that real Colchians behaved like Medea, or Phoenicians like the chorus of *Phoenissae*. Euripides' foreigners do not have the believable, concrete traits of the foreigners of Aeschylus and Sophocles. Like the myths in which they appear they have lost their historical reality. But together with the myth they have gained another kind of reality. Whether or not there is a Hades, the action of *Heracles* is a journey to and a rescue from a real Hell. Hippolytus rears in his own breast a team of uncontrollable horses that tear him apart. In the same way the barbarians who arouse the self-righteous contempt of Jason, Pentheus, Hermione, though they have no recognizable nationality, are real strangers. Nobly enduring, or wildly and cunningly vengeful, they are the types of the outsider, the exploitable caste, or nation, or sex, of every period. What this theme means in the plays of Euripides is material for a separate study.

APPENDIX

NAMES OF FOREIGN PEOPLES AND PLACES IN GREEK TRAGEDY

1. Catalogue of names used by Aeschylus, Sophocles, and Euripides

For the sake of simplicity I have adopted the following procedure. Under a given name are included all its derivatives, e.g., Egypt includes Egyptians, Troy includes Trojans, etc. I have omitted Hyperboreans, Hesperides, Gorgons, Phorcides, Sternophthalmi, Cynocephali, Lotus Eaters, Atlantides, as being more mythological than geographical. *Passim* after an entry means that the word occurs more than ten times in the play under consideration. *Title* indicates that a word, or one of its derivatives, occurs in a title. A capital letter A and a number following the title of a lost play of Euripides indicate a new fragment not listed in Nauck, e.g., under Asia, "*Hypsipyle* A 2." A stands for Allen and Italie. A full reference will be found in their *Concordance to Euripides*, under Asia. The number indicates that Asia, or a related word, is used twice in the new fragments of *Hypsipyle*.

Acesta — SOPH. fr. 611 *Hydrophoroi*

Adria — AESCH. fr. 71 *Heliades*
EUR. *Hipp.* 736

Aeria, another name for Egypt — AESCH. *Supp.* 75

Aetna — AESCH. *PV* 365; *title;* fr. 233 *Sisyphus Drapetes*
SOPH. *OC* 312; fr. 314 P *Ichneutae*, 300; fr. 165 *Daedalus*
EUR. *Cyc.* 20, 62, 95, 114, 130, 298, 366, 395, 599, 660; *Tro.* 220; *HF* 639

Agbatana — AESCH. *Pers.* 16, 535, 961

Aia, in Colchis — SOPH. fr. 828 inc.

Aiantia, a city of the Nabataians in Arabia — SOPH. fr. 896 inc.

Aithiops River — AESCH. *PV* 809

Amazons — AESCH. *PV* 723; *Eum.* 628, 685; *Supp.* 287
EUR. *Hipp.* 10, 307, 351, 581; *HF* 408; *Ion* 1145

Arabia — AESCH. *PV* 420. The text is uncertain.
EUR. *Bacch.* 16

Arians — AESCH. *Pers.* 994; *Cho.* 423

Arimaspians — AESCH. *PV* 805

Artace — SOPH. fr. 831 inc.

Asia	AESCH. *Supp.* 547; *Pers.* 12, 57, 61, 73, 249, 270, 549, 584, 763, 929; *PV* 412, 735; fr. 191 *PL* SOPH. *OC* 675; fr. 377 *Mysi* EUR. *Cyc.* 443; *Andr.* 1, 119; *Hec.* 481; *HF* 642; *Tro.* 748, 927, 1219; *Ion* 74, 1356, 1586; *El.* 315; *Or.* 353, 1397; *IT* 180, 396; *Bacch.* 17, 64, 1168; fr. 370 *Erechtheus;* fr. 981 inc. *Pirithous* A 1; *Hypsipyle* A 2
Atlantic	EUR. *Hipp.* 3, 1053; *HF* 234; fr. 145 *Andromeda;* fr. 594 *Pirithous*
Axine	EUR. *Andr.* 793; *HF* 410; *IT* 94, 125, 218, 253, 341, 395, 438, 1388
Axius River	AESCH. *Pers.* 493 EUR. *Bacch.* 569
Azeiotai	SOPH. fr. 146 *Achaion Sylloge*
Babylon	AESCH. *Pers.* 52
Bactria	AESCH. *Pers.* 306, 318, 732 EUR. *Bacch.* 15
Barca	SOPH. *El.* 727
Berecynthia	AESCH. fr. 158 *Niobe* SOPH. fr. 470 *Poimenes*
Bistones	EUR. *Alc.* 485, 1022
Bolbe Lake	AESCH. *Pers.* 494
Bosporus	AESCH. *Pers.* 723, 746 SOPH. *Ajax* 884; *Ant.* 969; fr. 462 *Poimenes;* fr. 641 *Phineus*
Byblus	AESCH. *Supp.* 761; *PV* 811 EUR. *Ion* 1195

Caecus River	AESCH. fr. 143, 144 *Mysi*
Canopus	AESCH. *Supp.* 310; *PV* 846
Caria	AESCH. *title;* fr. 99 *Cares* SOPH. fr. 497 *Salmoneus* EUR. *Cyc.* 654
Carthage	SOPH. fr. 545 *Triptolemus*
Caucasus	AESCH. *PV* 422, 719; fr. 193 *PL*
Celaenae	EUR. fr. 1085 inc.
Cerberian = Cimmerian	SOPH. fr. 957 inc.
Chaldaeans	SOPH. fr. 581 *Tympanistae*
Chalybes	AESCH. *Sept.* 728; *PV* 715 EUR. *Alc.* 980; fr. 472 *Cretes*
Charybdis = Strait of Messina	EUR. *Tro.* 436
Chryse	AESCH. *Pers.* 314 SOPH. fr. 37 *Aechmalotides;* fr. 353 *Lemniae*
Cilicia	AESCH. *Supp.* 551; *Pers.* 327; *PV* 351; *Cho.* 732 SOPH. fr. 181 *Helenes Apaitesis* EUR. fr. 819 *Phrixus*
Cilla	SOPH. fr. 37 *Aechmalotides*
Cimmeria	AESCH. *PV* 730
Cimmerian Bosporus	AESCH. *PV* 733
Cissia	AESCH. *Pers.* 17, 120; *Cho.* 423; fr. 405 inc. EUR. *Hec.* 3; fr. 229 *Archelaus*
Cisthene	AESCH. *PV* 793
Cnossus	SOPH. *Ajax* 698–700 EUR. *HF* 1327

Colchis	AESCH. *PV* 415 SOPH. *title;* fr. 581 *Tympanistae* EUR. *Medea* 2, 132
Cragos, in Lycia	EUR. fr. 669 *Stheneboia*
Crathis River	EUR. *Tro.* 228
Crete	AESCH. *Cho.* 616; *title;* fr. 187 *Penelope* SOPH. *Ajax* 1295; *Trach.* 119 EUR. *Hipp.* 156, 372, 719, 752, 757; *Tro.* 944; *Helen* 768; *Or.* 18, 1009; *Bacch.* 121; *title; title; Hypsipyle* A 1
Cyprus	AESCH. *Supp.* 282; *Pers.* 891 EUR. *Helen* 148; *Bacch.* 403
Edonians	AESCH. *Pers.* 495; *title* SOPH. *Ant.* 956 EUR. *Hec.* 1153; *Hypsipyle* A 1
Egypt	AESCH. *Supp.* 30, 817, 873, 1053; *Pers.* 35, 311; *title;* fr. 300, 373 inc. SOPH. *OC* 337; fr. 363 *Manteis;* fr. 646 *Phineus* EUR. *Tro.* 128; *El.* 1281; *Helen* 2, 5, 460, 461, 682
Enetoi	EUR. *Hipp.* 231, 1132
Eridanus	AESCH. fr. 73 *Heliades* EUR. *Hipp.* 737; cf. also Aesch. fr. 73
Erytheia	EUR. *HF* 425
Erythraean Sea = the Persian Gulf	AESCH. fr. 192 *PL*
Ethiopia	AESCH. *Supp.* 286; fr. 192 *PL;* fr. 300, 328, 329 inc. SOPH. *title*

Ethiopia	EUR. fr. 228 *Archelaus;* fr. 349 *Erechtheus*
Euxine	EUR. *Andr.* 1262
Gabioi = Abioi	AESCH. fr. 196 *PL*
Getai	SOPH. fr. 547 *Triptolemus*
Gulf of Rhea = Ionian Sea	AESCH. *PV* 837
Halys River	AESCH. *Pers.* 865
Hebrus River	EUR. *HF* 387
Hellespont	AESCH. *Pers.* 745 SOPH. fr. 462 *Poimenes*
Hierapolis or Cronia	AESCH. fr. 11 *Aetnaeae*
Himera	AESCH. fr. 32 *Glaucus Potnieus*
Hybristes River	AESCH. *PV* 717
Iberia	AESCH. fr. 73 *Heliades*
Ida in Crete	EUR. *Hipp.* 1253; fr. 471 *Cretes*
Ida in Troad	AESCH. *Ag.* 281, 283, 311, 564; fr. 158, 162, 163 *Niobe* SOPH. *Ajax* 434, 601; fr. 337 *Kophoi Satyroi;* fr. 469, 479 *Poimenes;* fr. 334 *Laocoon* EUR. *Andr.* 274, 294, 706; *Hec.* 325, 354, 631, 644, 944; *Tro.* 199, 976, 1067; *El.* 317; *Helen* 24, 29, 658, 1324, 1508; *Or.* 1364, 1380, 1383, 1453; *IA* 76, 575, 1284, 1287, 1288; fr. 471 *Cretes;* fr. 586 *Palamedes;* fr. 1085 inc.
Idean Dactyls	SOPH. fr. 337 *Kophoi Satyroi*
Ilium	AESCH. *Ag.* passim; *Cho.* 345; *Eum.* 457

Ilium	SOPH. *El.* 1; *Phil.* 7 EUR. *Cyc.* 107, 277, 281, 351; *Andr.* passim; *Hec.* passim; *Supp.* 1198; *Tro.* passim; *El.* 4, 452, 881, 1283; *IT* 12, 661, 1414; *Helen* passim; *Or.* 58, 78, 103, 648, 1361, 1381, 1508; *IA* 337, 755, 816, 965, 1261, 1312, 1475, 1510, 1520
Illyria	SOPH. fr. 544 *Triptolemus*
India	AESCH. *Supp.* 284 SOPH. *Ant.* 1037
Ionian Sea	EUR. *Phoen.* 208; *Tro.* 225
Ister River	AESCH. fr. 155 *Niobe;* fr. 197 *PL* SOPH. *OT* 1227
Italy	SOPH. *Ant.* 1119; fr. 543 *Triptolemus*
Kamikoi	SOPH. *title*
Leuke Akte	EUR. *Andr.* 1262; *IT* 436
Liburnians	AESCH. fr. 364 inc.
Libya	AESCH. *Supp.* 279, 317; *Eum.* 292; fr. 11 *Aetnaeae;* fr. 139 *Myrmidones* SOPH. *El.* 702 fr. 10 *Aias Lokros* EUR. *Alc.* 346; *HF* 684; *Tro.* 544; *Helen* 170, 404, 768, 1211, 1479; *Bacch.* 990; *IA* 1036; fr. 779 *Phaethon;* fr. 922 inc.
Liguria	AESCH. fr. 199 *PL* SOPH. fr. 541 *Triptolemus* EUR. *Tro.* 437
Lycia	AESCH. *Cho.* 346 EUR. *Alc.* 114

Lydia	AESCH. *Supp.* 550; *Pers.* 41, 770; fr. 59 *Edoni* SOPH. *Trach.* 70, 248, 356, 432; fr. 42 *Aechmalotides;* fr. 378 *Mysi;* fr. 732 inc. EUR. *Alc.* 675; *Bacch.* 13, 55, 140, 234, 464; *IA* 788
Lyrnessus	AESCH. *Pers.* 324; fr. 267 *Phryges*
Maeotis	AESCH. *PV* 418, 731 EUR. *HF* 409
Magians	AESCH. *Pers.* 318
Magnesia, on the Maeander	SOPH. fr. 963 inc.
Mardians	AESCH. *Pers.* 993
Mariandynia	AESCH. *Pers.* 51, 939
Media	AESCH. *Pers.* 236, 791 EUR. *Bacch.* 16
Memphis	AESCH. *Supp.* 310; *Pers.* 36
Mylasa	AESCH. fr. 101 *Cares*
Mysia	AESCH. *Supp.* 549; *Pers.* 52, 322, 1054; *title;* fr. 143 *Mysi* SOPH. *Ajax* 699, 720; *title;* fr. 377 *Mysi* EUR. fr. 476 *Licymnius;* fr. 704, 705 *Telephus; Telephus* A 5
Nile	AESCH. *Supp.* 4, 71, 281, 308, 497, 561, 880, 922, 1024; *Pers.* 34, 311; *PV* 812, 814, 847, 852; fr. 300 inc. SOPH. fr. 797 inc. EUR. *Andr.* 650; *Helen* 1, 89, 462, 491, 671; fr. 228 *Archelaus*

Nysa	SOPH. *Ant.* 731; fr. 874 inc. EUR. *Cyc.* 68; *Bacch.* 556
Oenotria	SOPH. fr. 541 *Triptolemus*
Pactolus River	SOPH. *Phil.* 394
Padus River	EUR. see Aesch. fr. 73
Paeonia	AESCH. *Supp.* 257
Pamphylia	AESCH. *Supp.* 552 SOPH. fr. 181 *Helenes Apaitesis*
Pangaeon Mt.	AESCH. *Pers.* 494 EUR. *Hypsipyle* A 1
Paphos	AESCH. *Pers.* 894 EUR. *Bacch.* 406
Percote	SOPH. fr. 831 inc.
Pergamum = Troy	EUR. *Tro.* 556, 1065, 1295; *IA* 773
Perseus' Rock, in Nile delta	EUR. *Helen* 769
Persia	AESCH. *Pers.* passim EUR. *Bacch.* 14
Phaeacia	SOPH. *title*
Pharos	EUR. *Helen* 5
Phasis River	AESCH. fr. 155 *Niobe;* fr. 191 *PL* SOPH. *OT* 1227 EUR. *Andr.* 651
Phlegraian Field	AESCH. *Eum.* 295 EUR. *HF* 1194; *Ion* 988
Phoenicia	AESCH. *Pers.* 410 SOPH. fr. 471 *Poimenes;* fr. 823 inc. EUR. *Tro.* 221; *Helen* 1151, 1272; *Phoen.* 6, 204, 246, 280, 301; fr. 472

Phoenicia — *Cretes;* fr. 819 *Phrixus; Hypsipyle* A 1

Phrygia — AESCH. *Supp.* 548; *Pers.* 770; *title;* fr. 446 inc.
SOPH. *Ajax* 210, 488, 1054, 1292; *Ant.* 824; *title;* fr. 337 *Kophoi Satyroi;* fr. 339 *Lacaenae;* fr. 344 *Laocoon;* fr. 378 *Mysi*
EUR. *Cyc.* 200, 284, 296; *Alc.* 675; *Andr.* 194, 204, 291, 363, 455, 592, 1044; *Hec.* 4, 350, 492, 776, 827, 1064, 1111, 1141; *Tro.* passim; *El.* 314, 336, 457, 681, 917 1001, 1281; *Helen* 39, 42, 109, 229, 369, 573, 608, 928; *Or.* passim; *Bacch.* 14, 58, 86, 127, 140, 159; *IA* passim; fr. 899 inc.; *Antiope* A 1; *Alexander* A 2

Pluto's Ford — AESCH. *PV* 806

Pontus = the Black Sea — AESCH. *Pers.* 72, 877; *PV* 726, 792
EUR. *Hipp.* 3, 1053

Propontis — AESCH. *Pers.* 876

Rhegium — AESCH. fr. 402 inc.

Rhipae — AESCH. fr. 68 *Heliades;* fr. 197 *PL*
SOPH. *OC* 1248

Salamis, in Cyprus — AESCH. *Pers.* 895
EUR. *Helen* 150

Salmydessus — AESCH. *PV* 726
SOPH. *Ant.* 970

Sardis — AESCH. *Pers.* 45, 321
SOPH. *Ant.* 1037
EUR. *Bacch.* 463; fr. 630 *Pleisthenes*

Sarpedonian Rock, in Cilicia or in Thrace(?)
AESCH. *Supp.* 869–70
SOPH. fr. 43 *Aechmalotides;* fr. 580 *Tympanistae*

Scamander — AESCH. *Ag.* 511, 1158; *Cho.* 366; *Eum.* 398
SOPH. *Ajax* 418
EUR. *Cyc.* 281; *Tro.* 29, 374, 1151; *Helen* 52, 368, 609; *Or.* 1310

Scythia — AESCH. *Sept.* 728, 818; *PV* 2, 417, 709; *Cho.* 161; *Eum.* 703; fr. 198 *PL*
SOPH. *title;* fr. 394 *Nauplius;* fr. 432 *Oenomaus;* fr. 641 *Phineus*

Sicels — EUR. *Cyc.* 95, 703; *Tro.* 222; *El.* 1347

Sicily — AESCH. *PV* 369; fr. 11 *Aetnaeae*
EUR. *Cyc.* 106, 114; *Phoen.* 211

Sidon — AESCH. *Supp.* 121, 132
SOPH. fr. 823 inc.
EUR. *Helen* 1413, 1451, 1531; *Bacch.* 171, 1025; fr. 819 *Phrixus*

Sigeum — SOPH. *Phil.* 335; *Ant.* 825

Simois — AESCH. *Ag.* 696
EUR. *Andr.* 1019, 1183; *Hec.* 642; *Tro.* 810, 1116; *El.* 441; *Helen* 250; *Or.* 809; *IA* 751, 767

Sipylus Mt. — AESCH. fr. 163 *Niobe*
SOPH. *Ant.* 825
EUR. *IA* 952

Skombroi, a Thracian tribe — SOPH. fr. 991 inc.

Soloi — AESCH. *Pers.* 894

Sousa	AESCH. *Pers.* 16, 119, 535, 557, 643, 730, 761
Strymon River	AESCH. *Supp.* 255; *Pers.* 497, 867; *Ag.* 192
Symplegades	EUR. *Medea* 2, 432, 1263; *Andr.* 794, 864; *IT* 124–5, 241, 260, 355, 392–5, 746, 1389
Syria	AESCH. *Supp.* 5; *Pers.* 84; *Ag.* 1312 SOPH. fr. 581 *Tympanistae* EUR. *Bacch.* 144
Taurians	EUR. *IT* 30, 85, 1454
Teuthrania	AESCH. *Supp.* 549 EUR. fr. 476 *Licymnius*
Thebe	EUR. *Andr.* 1
Thebes, in Egypt	AESCH. *Pers.* 38
Themiscyra	AESCH. *PV* 724
Thermodon	AESCH. *PV* 725
Thrace	AESCH. *Pers.* 509, 566, 870; *Ag.* 654, 1418; *title* SOPH. *Ant.* 589, 969; *OT* 197; fr. 216 *Thamyras;* fr. 523 *Tereus* EUR. *Cyc.* 329; *Alc.* 67, 483, 498, 967, 1021; *Andr.* 215; *Hec.* passim; fr. 360, 369 *Erechtheus; Hypsipyle* A 5
Thracian Chersonese	EUR. *Hec.* 8, 33
Tmolus Mt.	AESCH. *Pers.* 49 EUR. *Bacch.* 55, 65, 154, 462
Tritonis Lake	AESCH. *Eum.* 293 EUR. *Ion* 872

Troy	AESCH. *Ag.* passim; *Choe.* 304, 363; *Eum.* 457; fr. 99 *Cares;* fr. 296 inc. SOPH. *Ajax* passim; *El.* 1; *Phil.* passim; *title;* fr. 141 *Achaion Sylloge* EUR. *Cyc.* 107, 177, 198, 347, 603, 694, 698; *Andr.* passim; *Hec.* passim; *Tro.* passim; *El.* passim; *Helen* passim, *Or.* passim; *IT* 139, 517, 531; *IA* passim; fr. 935, 1082 inc.; *Alexander* A 1
Tyre	AESCH. *Pers.* 963 EUR. *Phoen.* 202, 639; *Hypsipyle* A 1
Tyrrhenia	AESCH. *Eum.* 567 SOPH. *Ajax* 17; fr. 248 *Inachus;* fr. 541 *Triptolemus* EUR. *Cyc.* 11; *Medea* 1342, 1359; *Heracl.* 830; *Phoen.* 1377
Xiphiros	AESCH. fr. 33 *Glaucus Potnieus.* The text is uncertain.

2. Distribution of names between extant plays and fragments

	AESCHYLUS	SOPHOCLES	EURIPIDES
no. of names used	100	61	77
no. of names not occurring in other two writers	39	21	22
no. of names in fragments	39	47	27
proportion of names in fragments	more than ⅓	more than ¾	less than ⅓
no. of names in fragments only	19	32	8
proportion of names in fragments only	about ⅕	about ½	about ⅒

3. *Distribution of names in extant plays*

The first number indicates the number of names used in a given play, the second number the total number of times that names of foreign peoples or places are used in a play. Words which are designated *passim* in the catalogue are counted as 10+. A total with one plus sign after it contains one such word, a total with two plus signs after it contains two such words, and so forth.

AESCHYLUS

Supp.	23	26
Pers.	42	85+
PV	24	34
Sept.	2	3
Ag.	9	31++
Cho.	9	10
Eum.	9	10

SOPHOCLES

Ajax	9	25+
Trach.	2	5
Ant.	9	12
OT	3	3
El.	4	4
Phil.	4	13+
OC	4	4
Ich.	1	1

EURIPIDES

Cyc.	12	34
Alc.	7	12
Medea	3	7
Hipp.	8	18
Heracl.	1	1
Andr.	13	42++
Supp.	1	1
HF	10	10
Hec.	11	51+++
Tro.	17	54+++
El.	8	26+
IT	7	27
Helen	16	64++
Phoen.	4	10
Ion	5	7
Or.	8	36++
Bacch.	17	31
IA	9	40++

These figures give a rough measurement of the difference in usage between Aeschylus and Euripides. Euripides' foreign plays have, on the whole, few names often repeated—a sign of their formulaic and thematic function. It has been suggested (e.g., by Krausse, *De Euripide Aeschyli instauratore*, pp. 206–9) that the chorus of *Phoenissae* is an attempt to emulate Aeschylus' barbarian choruses, but the figures for *Phoenissae* (4 names used 10 times) as compared with those for Aeschylus' *Suppliants* (23 names used 36 times) show how much less Euripides' chorus are concerned with the foreign land from which they have come. Not much can be inferred from the figures for Sophocles, since we have seen (p. 112 above) that his extant plays are probably not representative of his method of treating foreigners. *Agamemnon* and *Ajax* approximate the Euripidean pattern of repetitions, though on a much smaller scale. This is because of the recurrence of names for Troy in these plays.

BIBLIOGRAPHY

1. Editions of ancient authors

AESCHYLUS

Aeschyli septem quae supersunt tragoediae, ed. Gilbert Murray, Oxford, Clarendon, 1937.

Tragedies, ed. F. Paley, London, 1855.

Aeschyli tragoediae, ed. H. Weil, Leipzig, 1852.

Agamemnon, ed. Eduard Fraenkel, Oxford, Clarendon, 1950.

Suppliants, ed. Johannes Oberdick, Berlin, 1869.

EURIPIDES

Euripidis fabulae, ed. Gilbert Murray, 3 vols. Oxford, Clarendon, n.d.

Euripidis tragoediae, fragmenta, epistolae, ed. Samuel Musgrave, 3 vols. Leipzig, 1788.

Works, with an English Commentary, ed. F. A. Paley, 2nd ed. 3 vols. London, 1872–8.

Bacchae, ed. E. R. Dodds, 2nd ed. Oxford, Clarendon, 1960.

Ion, ed. A. S. Owen, Oxford, Clarendon, 1939.

Ion, ed. Ulrich von Wilamowitz-Moellendorff, Berlin, Weidmann, 1926.

SOPHOCLES

Sophoclis fabulae, ed. A. C. Pearson, 2nd ed. Oxford, Clarendon, 1923.

The Fragments of Sophocles, ed. A. C. Pearson, 3 vols. Cambridge University Press, 1917.

Tragicorum Graecorum fragmenta, ed. A. Nauck, 2nd ed. Leipzig, B. G. Teubner, 1889.

2. *General reference works*

Allen, James T., Gabriel Italie, *A Concordance to Euripides*, Berkeley and Los Angeles, University of California Press, 1954.

Boisacq, Émile, *Dictionnaire Étymologique de la Langue Grecque*, 4th ed. Heidelberg, C. Winter, 1950.

Daremberg, Ch., Edm. Saglio, *Dictionnaire des Antiquités Grecques et Romaines d'après les Textes et Monuments*, Paris, Hachette, 1877–1919.

Ellendt, F., *Lexicon Sophocleum*, 2nd ed. Berlin, Borntraeger, 1872.

Frisk, Hjalmar, *Griechisches etymologisches Wörterbuch*, fascicles 1–9, Heidelberg, C. Winter, 1954–9.

Italie, Gabriel, *Index Aeschyleus*, Leiden, E. J. Brill, 1955.

The Oxford Classical Dictionary, ed. M. Cary, J. D. Denniston, J. Wight Duff, A. D. Nock, W. D. Ross, H. H. Scullard with the assistance of H. J. Rose, H. P. Harvey, A. Souter, Oxford, Clarendon, 1949.

Real-Encyclopädie der classischen Altertumswissenschaft, ed. A. Pauly, G. Wissowa, W. Kroll, Stuttgart, Alfred Druckenmüller, 1894– .

Schmid, Wilhelm, Otto Stählin, *Geschichte der griechischen Literatur*, Part I, 5 vols. Munich, C. H. Beck, 1929–48.

3. Books, monographs, articles

Alföldi, Andreas, "Gewaltherrscher und Theaterkönig," *Late Classical and Mediaeval Studies in Honor of Albert Mathias Friend Jr.*, ed. Kurt Weitzman and others (Princeton University Press, 1955), pp. 15–55.

Bates, W. N., *Euripides, a Student of Human Nature*, Philadelphia, University of Pennsylvania Press, 1930.

Bowra, C. M., *Problems in Greek Poetry*, Oxford, Clarendon, 1953.

Butler, H. C., *Sardis; Publications of the American Society for the Excavation of Sardis*, vol. 1, part 2, Leyden, E. J. Brill, 1922– .

Collinge, N. E., "Euripides' *Hecuba* 925–6," *Classical Philology*, *49* (1954), 35–6.

Degen, H., *De Troianis scaenicis*, diss. Leipzig, 1900.

Diller, Aubrey, *Race Mixture among the Greeks before Alexander* (Illinois Studies in Language and Literature, *20*), Urbana, University of Illinois Press, 1937.

Dodds, E. R., "Maenadism in the *Bacchae*," *Harvard Theological Review*, *33* (1940), 155–76.

Dunkel, H. B., *Panhellenism in Greek Tragedy*, diss. Chicago, 1937.

Earp, F. R., *The Style of Aeschylus*, Cambridge University Press, 1948.

Earp, F. R., *The Style of Sophocles*, Cambridge University Press, 1944.

Eichorn, Arno, *βάρβαρος quid significaverit*, diss. Leipzig, 1904.

Farnell, L. R., *Cults of the Greek States*, 5 vols. Oxford, Clarendon, 1896–1909.

Friedländer, Paul, *Die griechische Tragödie und das Tragische*, Part 3, "Die Antike," 2 (1926), pp. 76–112.

Gow, A. S. F., "Notes on the *Persae* of Aeschylus," *Journal of Hellenic Studies*, *48* (1928), 133–58.

Greenwood, Sam Lee, *Geographical Allusion in Attic Tragedy*, diss. Chicago, 1938.

Griffith, John G., "Some Thoughts on 'Helena' of Euripides," *Journal of Hellenic Studies*, *73* (1953), 36–41.

Havelock, E. A., *The Crucifixion of Intellectual Man*, Boston, Beacon Press, 1951.

Hofman, Hans Herman, *Über den Zusammenhang zwischen Chorliedern und Handlung in den erhaltenen Dramen des Euripides*, diss. Leipzig, 1916.

Jüthner, Julius, *Hellenen und Barbaren, aus der Geschichte des Nationalbewusstseins* (Das Erbe des Alten, new series, vol. 8), Leipzig, Dieterich, 1923.

Kranz, W., *Stasimon*, Berlin, Weidmann, 1933.

Krausse, O., *De Euripide Aeschyli instauratore*, diss. Jena, 1905.

Lattimore, Richmond, "Aeschylus on the Defeat of Xerxes," *Classical Studies in Honor of William Abbott Oldfather* (Urbana, 1943), pp. 82–93.

Miller, Walter, *Daedalus and Thespis, The Contributions of the Ancient Dramatic Poets to Our Knowledge of the Arts and Crafts of Greece*, 3 vols. New York, Macmillan, 1929–32.

Nestle, W., "Untersuchungen über die philosophischen Quellen des Euripides," *Philologus*, suppl. 8 (1901), 557–655.

Norden, E., *Die Geburt des Kindes*, Leipzig, B. G. Teubner, 1924.

Parke, H. W., D. E. W. Wormell, *The Delphic Oracle*, 2 vols. Oxford, B. Blackwell, 1956.

Pearson, A. C., "The *Rhesus*," *Classical Review, 35* (1921), 52–61.

Petersen, E., "Andromeda," *Journal of Hellenic Studies, 24* (1904), 99–112.

Pohlenz, Max, *Griechische Tragödie*, 2nd ed. 2 vols. Göttingen, Vandenhoeck and Ruprecht, 1954.

Post, C. R., *The Dramatic Art of Sophocles as Revealed by the Fragments of the Lost Plays* (Harvard Studies in Classical Philology, *33*), Cambridge, Harvard University Press, 1922, pp. 1–63.

Pritchard, James B., *Ancient Near Eastern Texts Relating to the Old Testament*, 2nd ed. Princeton University Press, 1955.

Rasch, J., *Sophocles quid debeat Herodoto in rebus ad fabulas exornandas adhibitis* (Commentationes Philologicae Jenenses, *10*), Leipzig, B. G. Teubner, 1913.

Richter, G. M. A., *Greek Painting, The Metropolitan Museum of Art*, 4th ed. New York, 1952.

Roth, Friederich, *Bemerkungen über den Sinn und Gebrauch des Wortes Barbar*, diss. Nürnberg, 1814.

Schmid, W., *Untersuchungen zum gefesselten Prometheus* (Tübinger Beiträge zur Altertumswissenschaft, *9*), Stuttgart, W. Kohlhammer, 1929.

Schmidt, J. H. Heinrich, *Die Eurythmie in den Chorgesängen der Griechen*, Leipzig, 1868.

Snell, Bruno, "Aischylos und das Handeln im Drama," *Philologus*, suppl. 20 (1928), 1–164.

Snell, Bruno, *The Discovery of the Mind*, trans. T. G. Rosenmeyer, Oxford, B. Blackwell, 1953.

Stanford, W. B., *Aeschylus in His Style, A Study in Language and Personality*, Dublin, the University Press, 1942.

Stanford, W. B., "Traces of Sicilian Influence in Aeschylus," *Proceedings of the Royal Irish Academy*, *44*, C8 (1937–8), 229–40.

Studniczka, F., *Beiträge zur Geschichte der altgriechischen Tracht* (Abhandlungen des archäologisch-epigraphischen Seminares der Universität Wien, *6*, 1), Vienna, C. Gerold's Sohn, 1886, pp. 1–143.

Webster, T. B. L., *Greek Theatre Production*, London, Methuen, 1956.

Welcker, F. G., *Die griechischen Tragödien*, 3 vols. Bonn, 1839–41.

Wells, Joseph, *Studies in Herodotus*, Oxford, B. Blackwell, 1923.

Werner, Hans, "Barbarus," *Neue Jahrbuch für das klassische Altertum*, *41* (1918), 389–408.

Whitman, Cedric, *Sophocles, a Study in Heroic Humanism*, Cambridge, Harvard University Press, 1951.

Wilamowitz-Moellendorff, Ulrich von, *Aischylos Interpretationen*, Berlin, Weidmann, 1914.

Wilamowitz-Moellendorff, Ulrich von, *Einleitung in die attische Tragödie*, Berlin, Weidmann, 1889.

Wilamowitz-Moellendorff, Ulrich von, "Lesefrüchte," *Hermes*, *61* (1926), 281–9, and *62* (1927), 283–8.

Wilamowitz-Moellendorff, Ulrich von, "Die Spürhunde des Sophokles," *Neue Jahrbücher für das klassische Altertum Geschichte und deutsche Literatur*, *29* (1912), 449–76.

INDEX OF QUOTATIONS AND REFERENCES TO THE PLAYS

Numbers in italics indicate lines or fragments quoted

SOPHOCLES

EURIPIDES

Designed by Crimilda Pontes,
set in Janson type, with hand-lettered titles,
and printed by the Vail-Ballou Press, Inc.,
Binghamton, New York.